T0049568

METAPHYSICAL AF

METAPHYSICAL

AF

HARNESS YOUR DREAMS IN THE ETHEREAL REALM

MAGGIE WILSON

STERLING ETHOS

New York

STERLING ETHOS
New York

ISBN 978-1-4549-5244-2
ISBN 978-1-4549-5245-9 (e-book)

Library of Congress Control Number: 2023948383

For information about custom editions, special sales, and premium purchases,
please contact specialsales@unionsquareandco.com.

Printed in the United States of America

2 4 6 8 10 9 7 5 3 1

unionsquareandco.com

Cover design by Jo Obarowski
Interior design by Kevin Ullrich
Cover and interior art by Aurore Thill, © 2024 Union Square & Co., LLC, except
for images by Shutterstock.com: Dream01: p. 24; Anastasiia Usenko: p. 52

For my children, Aurora and Achilles, who taught me about real magic.

CONTENTS

INTRODUCTION

A Metaphysical Odyssey

Step into a realm where the boundaries of the known dissolve and the universe unveils its deepest mysteries. Welcome to the extraordinary world of metaphysics, where we dare to venture beyond the physical and embrace the wonders of the unknown and the unseen. As my great friend Nina always says, "The sky is our jumping-off point." With that boundless spirit, we embark on a fascinating and interactive journey of exploration.

In this book we will delve into the depths of metaphysics, the study of all things beyond the ordinary. Learning about this subject means being willing to be transformed. Take the time to approach these quantum rituals, dimensional blueprints, and frequency downloads from a place of openness, with the full knowledge that they may ignite your mind and heart. This is not just about manifesting, or understanding the quantum field, or working with plant spirits, although we'll cover all those topics. What this book is all about is more than that: it's about unleashing the power within you to shape your reality every single day.

Together, we will unravel the threads of fear-driven separation and embrace life as creators. We'll engage with ancient wisdom, modern insights, and our own intuitive knowing, merging them into a harmonious mindset that will help you understand yourself more deeply so that you can create a reality that awakens your own limitless potential.

Let's journey through this universe together and find the keys to unlocking the secrets that are held in your DNA, in your genetic makeup—the ones that can transform your very being. Extraordinary discoveries await those who dare to explore the cosmos within and without! Just be sure to keep a few things in mind as you begin.

Be Kind to Yourself

Metaphysics isn't about repeating the same mantra that you can't bring yourself to actually believe. You'll know if the words you're repeating feel flat. If you say them a million times but aren't believing them, they'll change nothing, because you haven't created the space for the actual change to happen in your life. You won't be ready to hold that energy. Remember, you are your own cocreation with the universe. And the first step to having a metaphysical mindset is to make sure both you and the universe are working *for* you, not against you. So move beyond your cynical mind, create space for change (more on that later!), and commit to the process with an open heart.

Living Metaphysical

Being mindful is one thing, but having a metaphysical mindset is another. In this book I will show you how to bring the "meta-physical" into your reality. "Meta" means "beyond," and I intend to give you quantum tools to get beyond enlightenment and into a life that is as metaphysical as fuck.

I won't tell you how you must change. Instead, I encourage you to remember who you have always been: divine, joyful, powerful, and truly free. I hope the words in this book make moving through your daily life with the knowledge of a world beyond this one effortless and powerful.

If you also have *The Metaphysical Cannabis Oracle Deck*, you'll see that there are ties to some cards and the messages that are in them. Each card in the metaphysical cannabis oracle deck has a deeper understanding. Those cards that stand out the most that don't have the longest descriptions are concepts that couldn't be properly described in a short guidebook. *The Metaphysical Cannabis Oracle Deck* is a brilliant companion to this book, and you will do readings and have daily journal prompts if you continue to use this book and the deck in unison.

PART 1
What Is a Metaphysical Mindset?

"A habit is a redundant set of automatic, unconscious thoughts, behaviors, and emotions that you gain through frequent repetition."

—Tchiki Davis, *The Berkeley Well-Being Institute*

Welcome to *Metaphysical AF*, a transformative exploration into the depths of metaphysical thought and spiritual awakening. In this captivating journey, we will dive into the realms of consciousness, energy, and interconnectedness, seeking profound truths that transcend the boundaries of our material existence. Part 1 lays the foundation for your voyage, equipping you with the tools to embrace a metaphysical mindset and delve into the wonders that lie beyond the veil of perception.

In this section, we will embark on a historical expedition, tracing the origins of metaphysics through the ages. As we embark on this journey of metaphysical awakening, prepare to challenge your perceptions, expand your consciousness, and connect with the profound wisdom that has guided seekers throughout the ages. Part 1 is your gateway to embracing a deeper understanding of reality and embarking on a path of self-discovery that transcends the ordinary. So buckle up and get ready to embark on this enlightening adventure—the beginning of your journey toward becoming Metaphysical AF!

CHAPTER 1

LEARNING FROM THE PAST

T hroughout history, metaphysics has been a captivating field of inquiry that seeks to unravel the fundamental nature of reality, existence, and the cosmos. It encompasses a wide array of philosophical, spiritual, and mystical beliefs that have evolved over the ages. From ancient civilizations to modern times, thinkers, philosophers, and scholars have engaged in profound contemplations and discussions about the nature of reality and our place in the universe. Here is just a quick overview of how our understanding of metaphysics has changed throughout time and around the world.

Ancient Eastern Wisdom

In ancient civilizations like India and China, metaphysical thought took root in sacred texts and philosophical treatises. The Upanishads, part of the Vedic scriptures in Hinduism, delve into the nature of the self (called *Atman*) and its connection to the universal consciousness (*Brahman*). The *Bhagavad Gita,* a revered Hindu scripture, explores the paths to spiritual liberation and the cosmic order. In Chinese philosophy, the *Tao Te Ching* by Lao Tzu expounds the principles of the *Tao*, the natural order of the universe, emphasizing the importance of harmony, balance, and simplicity in life.

Greek Philosophical Foundations

In ancient Greece, metaphysical exploration blossomed with the works of philosophers such as Plato and Aristotle. Plato's dialogues, particularly *The Republic* and *Timaeus,* investigated the nature of reality, knowledge, and the forms. Aristotle's *Metaphysics* examined the principles of being, substance, and causality. These foundational texts laid the groundwork for metaphysical inquiry in the Western world.

Medieval Synthesis of Faith and Reason

During the Middle Ages, metaphysics intertwined with religious and theological perspectives. Christian theologians like St. Augustine of Hippo, in his seminal work *Confessions,* explored the nature of God, the soul, and divine grace. Thomas Aquinas, in *Summa Theologica,* presented a comprehensive synthesis of Christian theology and Aristotelian metaphysics.

Renaissance Rationalism and Enlightenment

The Renaissance and Enlightenment eras marked a shift toward rationalism and empiricism. Renowned thinkers like René Descartes, in *Meditations on First Philosophy,* sought to establish a foundation for knowledge through doubt and reason. Spinoza's *Ethics* explored the concept of God as the immanent and infinite substance, while Leibniz's *Monadology* delved into the nature of reality as composed of indivisible monads.

Transcendentalism and Idealism

In the nineteenth century, transcendentalist thinkers like Ralph Waldo Emerson and Henry David Thoreau in works such as "Self-Reliance" and *Walden* embraced individual intuition, nature, and spiritual interconnectedness. Meanwhile, German idealists like Immanuel Kant, in *Critique of Pure Reason,* and Georg Wilhelm Friedrich Hegel, in *Phenomenology of Spirit,* explored the relationship between consciousness, mind, and reality.

Modern and Contemporary Explorations

In the twentieth century, metaphysics continued to evolve with advances in physics and psychology. Albert Einstein's theory of relativity revolutionized our understanding of space, time, and gravity, contributing to philosophical reflections on the nature of the universe. Carl Jung's exploration of the collective unconscious and archetypes expanded metaphysical inquiries into the depths of the human psyche.

Contemporary philosophers and writers like Alan Watts (*The Book: On the Taboo Against Knowing Who You Are*) and Ken Wilber (*A Brief History of Everything*) have bridged metaphysical concepts with modern science and psychology. They explore themes of interconnectedness, consciousness, and the evolution of human understanding.

The history of metaphysics is a rich tapestry of diverse perspectives, beliefs, and inquiries into the nature of reality. From ancient Eastern wisdom to Western philosophical developments and contemporary explorations, metaphysics continues to inspire seekers and thinkers worldwide.

Why Do We Study Metaphysics?

The exploration of the past in metaphysics provides valuable insights and perspectives that can help us prepare to cultivate a metaphysical mindset. Understanding the historical development of metaphysical thought offers several benefits:

1. Rich Heritage of Ideas: The history of metaphysics showcases a vast array of philosophical, spiritual, and mystical ideas from different cultures and periods. By studying this heritage, we gain exposure to diverse perspectives and can draw inspiration from the profound insights of ancient wisdom and modern reflections.

2. Integration of Wisdom: Learning from the past allows us to integrate timeless wisdom into our contemporary understanding. The accumulated knowledge of generations of thinkers can provide us with a comprehensive foundation for approaching metaphysical concepts and dilemmas in our own lives.

3. Contextual Understanding: Examining the historical context of metaphysical ideas helps us appreciate how societal, cultural, and intellectual influences have shaped different beliefs and viewpoints. Understanding the context can help us approach metaphysical questions with a nuanced and tolerant mindset.

4. Identification of Patterns: Observing recurring themes and ideas throughout history helps us recognize universal truths

and enduring questions about the natures of reality, consciousness, and existence. Identifying these patterns can deepen our contemplations and encourage us to seek our own understanding of these fundamental concepts.

5. Relevance to Contemporary Life: The exploration of the past helps us see the enduring relevance of metaphysical concepts in our modern lives. Many age-old questions about purpose, meaning, and interconnectedness remain pertinent, and the wisdom of the past can offer insights to guide our personal and spiritual growth.

6. Inspiration for Personal Transformation: The stories of ancient and modern thinkers who grappled with metaphysical questions can serve as inspiration for our own journeys of self-discovery and transformation. Understanding their struggles, breakthroughs, and perspectives can encourage us to embark on our unique path to developing a metaphysical mindset.

7. Grounding in Traditions: For those who find resonance in specific philosophical or spiritual traditions, exploring the historical foundations of metaphysics can provide a sense of grounding and belonging within those traditions. This sense of belonging can foster a deeper commitment to understanding and embracing the core principles of a metaphysical mindset.

Ultimately, the study of metaphysics empowers us to develop a more open, inquisitive, and contemplative approach to life. It encourages us to explore the mysteries of existence, connect with our inner selves, and embrace a broader understanding of the interconnectedness of all things. As we engage with the past, we gain the tools and perspectives to prepare ourselves for the transformative journey toward adopting a metaphysical mindset in our present lives.

Other Branches to Consider

If you are interested in metaphysics, you might be interested in one or more of the following: meditation, astrology, ESP, mysticism, reincarnation, life after death, Jungian psychology, philosophy, dreams, the egocentric philosophy—the list goes on. These might seem like disparate subjects, but the common factor is that they all deal with an exploration of reality, or the shared sense of reality we have as individuals as well as a society. If you're interested in metaphysics as a philosophical concept, it just means that you want to expand your mind: you are someone who seeks purpose, a meaning in life, and truth. So I encourage you to look into all the varied ways you can pursue that! This book will give you some general hints, but there is a whole world of inquiry available to you. In some locations there are even schools for such pursuits. For example, in Sedona, Arizona, there is a University of Metaphysics at which you can get a doctoral degree in the subject. And new things are being discovered in this field every day. So don't limit yourself—take this book as a guide, but remember that we are understanding more and more that science can't be our only basis for understanding our place in this world. To see it as more of a mirror of our own experience, give yourself the tools to go deeper.

CHAPTER 2

WHAT IS A METAPHYSICAL MINDSET?

According to Oxford Languages, a mindset is "the established set of attitudes held by someone." In other words, it's how a person usually thinks.

A metaphysical mindset, however, is a bit more complicated. Having a metaphysical mindset means embracing a perspective about life that goes beyond the surface of reality and delves into the unseen, the mystical, and the interconnected aspects of existence. It involves being open-minded and receptive to exploring new concepts that transcend the material world, such as spirituality, consciousness, energy, and the true potential of the human mind.

But what's the difference between a metaphysical mindset and one that is not? The answer lies in the way we perceive and interpret the world around us. The way most of us tend to see the world focuses primarily on the physical realm and relies on empirical evidence and logic to understand reality. While this approach is essential for practical matters, it also limits our understanding of the deeper layers of existence and the true interconnectedness of all things.

A metaphysical mindset allows us to tap into the wonders of the unseen. By embracing the idea that there is more to reality than meets the eye, we can experience several remarkable benefits, including expanded consciousness, heightened intuition, spiritual growth, enhanced creativity, greater empathy, more compassion, and inner peace. The beauty of this way of experiencing the world is that it is not limited to any particular group or belief system. Anyone open to exploring the mysteries of their own existence, willing to question the status quo, and receptive to the idea that there might be more to reality than what is readily apparent can benefit from a metaphysical mindset. In essence, a metaphysical mindset opens the door to extraordinary moments, fostering a deeper understanding of the self, the universe, and our place within it. It is an invitation to embark on a journey of exploration and discovery, where the boundaries of ordinary existence dissolve and the magic of the unseen becomes a wondrous reality.

Inputs and Outputs

First, take the time to look at the way you currently live: the patterns that occur again and again, and the emotions and thoughts that you habitually have. You are, in fact, a biological computer, and the first thing that you need to understand in order to inhabit a metaphysical way of thinking is that what you input and output matters. From the thoughts you think, to the beliefs you continue to tell yourself, to how you were raised and every trauma you've ever experienced, it all lives in the hard drive of your body. When you have an awareness of these things, you can decipher which programs you want to keep and which ones you want to uninstall.

By the end of this book, you will have an understanding of why you're running the programs you run, and will be able to make independent choices about how to reprogram yourself to create real, physical change.

Everything that we seek outside of ourselves, whether through reading books, studying the tarot, using psychedelics, or even binge-watching Esther Hicks videos—all of this represents a belief that you are going to find relief outside of yourself. I hope that, with this book, we can all start working on a new mindset that represents a world in which we can look inside ourselves instead.

In Our DNA

My friend Nina and I once found ourselves deep in conversation, discussing the paradigm shift that we were both personally experiencing, from a mindset where we were seeking validation from the outside world to one in which we realized that everything we needed was already within us, innate and waiting to be tapped into. Nina said to me that she had once believed that she needed a huge amount of that validation in order to be worthy of the goodness, joy, and love that she desired. However, with her newfound understanding, she realized that worthiness already existed within her.

I chimed in to say that I had been through a similar shift, but that I had also recognized that many belief systems and societal structures condition us to feel unworthy and force us to constantly strive for validation. This is a struggle that is particularly present in marginalized populations, who have been intentionally manipulated to feel subordinate and unworthy. Healing and shifting these mindsets is far more complex than it theoretically ought to be, due to the generational traumas and systemic oppression ingrained in our DNA.

If this describes your experience, give yourself the space and understanding to recognize that you may be dealing with an additional set of obstacles. If you are dealing with the generational trauma that comes with being a part of a marginalized population, that doesn't mean a metaphysical mindset is beyond your reach. It just means that you will need to give yourself grace as you navigate this journey. And remember to marvel, like we did, at the power of the human mind and its potential. We use only a fraction of our brain's capacity, and so much of its power lies untapped and waiting to be explored.

Challenges and Responsibilities

Anyone who takes on the challenge of putting together the puzzle that is metaphysics should be commended. Our exploration empowers others to begin their own journeys. For this reason, this awareness comes with immense responsibility. Embracing a metaphysical mindset isn't only about personal transformation; it's also about breaking down oppressive systems and creating a world where everyone has the opportunity to access their innate power.

CHAPTER 3

THE LAWS OF THE UNIVERSE

U nderstanding the Laws of the Universe is the key to unlocking the power of cocreation and cultivating a metaphysical mindset. As we uncover various healing modalities, it becomes evident that these laws govern the very fabric of our existence. By grasping their principles, we gain the ability to navigate life's challenges, manifest our desires, and tap into our highest potential. This chapter explores the significance of aligning ourselves with these universal laws, empowering us to cocreate our reality and embrace a profound metaphysical perspective on life.

While you may not know all twelve universal laws, you may be familiar with the Law of Attraction. The bestselling book and movie *The Secret* and viral Reel and TikTok trends of using sound clips from Esther Hicks's live teachings have made these concepts mainstream and available to everyone with an Internet connection. But the Law of Attraction is actually the third universal law of twelve. And because all the laws build on each other, you'll need to understand all of them and how they correspond to each other in order to create the energy you'll need to raise your vibration and have what you want to come to you. These "laws" combine metaphysics, spirit, and science, so they can function like a mini travel guide for your spirit to use daily.

Science, Spirituality, and Metaphysics

Metaphysics is the branch of philosophy that delves into the fundamental nature of reality and existence. It explores concepts beyond the physical realm, such as consciousness, energy, and the nature of being. The laws of the universe, as understood in metaphysics, go beyond conventional scientific principles, acknowledging that there are unseen forces and dimensions that influence our lives.

Spirituality centers on the quest for meaning, purpose, and connection with something greater than ourselves. It encompasses beliefs about the soul, the afterlife, and the divine. The laws of the universe, when viewed through a spiritual lens, often align with the concept of cosmic intelligence or universal consciousness. Spirituality acknowledges that there is an inherent order and harmony in the universe, and that we are interconnected with all living beings.

Science is the empirical study of the natural world, using systematic observation, experimentation, and analysis to understand how the universe operates. While some aspects of metaphysics and spirituality may not be directly observable or measurable through scientific methods, certain universal laws have parallels in science. For instance, the Law of Energy Conservation in physics is akin to the metaphysical law that energy cannot be created or destroyed, only transformed. Additionally, the concept of interconnectedness in ecology aligns with the idea of oneness and interconnectedness in spiritual and metaphysical teachings. The convergence of these three realms—metaphysics, spirit, and science—reveals that the universe operates under a cohesive set of principles. It suggests that there is more to reality than what meets the eye, and the exploration of these laws opens the door to deeper insights and wisdom.

These principles can help us keep an open mind, providing guidance when we experience separation—in other words, when the voices in our heads tell us that we aren't in control or that things aren't going our way.

Journaling Practice

At the end of each section on the twelve laws, I will give you various ways to apply their principles in your everyday life. Let's start this transformative journey together with a powerful journal prompt. Grab a dedicated notebook, reserved solely for exploring your relationship with the universal law that we'll be delving into. Write down your initial thoughts, emotions, and reflections as you learn about this law and how it relates to your life. I'll also provide a phrase to meditate on as your daily gratitude, and another for reflection, to add an additional facet to your experience.

As you read each section, allow your understanding of the law to seep into your consciousness. Continue journaling for the first few days, or even throughout the first month, capturing the shifts and insights that arise within you. You might notice that your impressions and interpretations of the law evolve over time, deepening your connection to its wisdom.

This journaling practice is a remarkable way to witness how living each law influences your experiences. By aligning your thoughts and actions with these universal principles, you'll find yourself attracting positive energies and opportunities into your life. So let your words flow onto the pages, and embrace the wondrous journey of manifestation that awaits you!

Just remember, learning how to use these new tools is only the start of the journey. Once you apply these skills to the way you're living, you'll open yourself up to an unlimited number of opportunities. For those already familiar—or even somewhat acquainted—with these laws, welcome to the next phase of your journey! Embracing these universal principles is merely the beginning, as now you have the opportunity to deepen your understanding and refine your application of these transformative tools. As you explore their nuances and integrate them into your life, you'll unlock new levels of mastery, guiding you toward greater alignment, manifestation, and fulfillment. So let your curiosity and awareness guide you, as you continue to unfold the magic of these timeless laws. The adventure awaits!

The Laws

Read below for an overview of each of the laws of the universe, and then a section on how to apply them to your daily life as you shift to a metaphysical mindset.

The Law of Oneness

All the kingdoms of the world share one universal host: the planet itself. In other words, we are all sharing one existence as parts of the same organism. The first principle is a reminder that everything is connected. This breaks down to every word, choice, desire, thought—they all have an impact on our combined existence. And because everything you do has such a broad impact, you can consider the Law of Oneness to be a foundation for every interaction you have in life, from the people you see every day to everyone in the entire world. This knowledge can become a daily practice: if you wake up in the morning and the negative voices in your head are threatening to separate you from this oneness, allow yourself to be kinder. Treat yourself gently and push away that negativity with love. As we internalize the Law of Oneness, we experience a profound shift in our relationships. Instead of seeking validation and connection externally, we recognize that true fulfillment comes from nurturing our inner connection to ourselves and the universal consciousness. This inner alignment creates a sense of wholeness, allowing us to approach relationships from a place of genuine love, support, and authenticity.

This can expand into seeing others who you interact with during the day with more compassion, which can mean not letting something get on your nerves or under your skin as much as it typically would.

When the Law of Oneness becomes an intentional practice, you become hyper-aware that the waves of energy, the masses of particles flowing from your body, and the way you feel around others and yourself matters. And when you pay close attention to the energies surrounding others, you can decipher or "read a room" extremely well. It is undeniable that we possess the ability to sense and intuitively perceive when something is amiss with others. But remember to tap in to that oneness when you are attempting to intuit energy, whether in a person, place, or situation. A popular trend suggests that you seek out "good vibes" or positive thoughts only; that when something "doesn't align with your energy," it's bad. The Law of Oneness helps us remember that good and bad are subjective, originating from each person's perspective. When you think about how the whole doesn't want a piece of itself to die because then the whole itself would diminish, it makes you realize that every single act of compassion counts. Kindness is the root at the Law of Oneness.

Imagine how powerful your mind has the potential to be when your actions are in line with this first law. When the lower energies of fear and anger aren't impeding how you go through your day-to-day, you create a powerful shift that opens the door to more optimistic opportunities. Fear and anger, often rooted in negativity and discord, can act as barriers, hindering personal growth and attracting undesirable outcomes. However, by consciously releasing these lower vibrations and embracing higher energies, you pave the way for a brighter, more harmonious reality.

Little miracles keep popping up not because you are lucky, but because you are tapping into a universal principle. Remember, your body is a bio-computer with a magnet at its center: your heart. When the heart becomes bitter and angry, it still maintains its magnetic charge. It doesn't lose the charge until it stops beating. The charge intensifies when you fall in love, when there's adrenaline running through your veins, and when you're consumed by fear or jealousy. It is broadcasting at a low frequency, which perpetuates this cycle by bringing more of the same energy to you.

I can give you an amazing example of how connected you can stay with someone when the universe wills it to be that way. When I was seven years old, I lived in a small town in southeast Tennessee. In Mrs. Hemphill's first-grade class, I met a little redhead named Stephanie. She was short with freckles, and we used to sit together singing Hanson's "MMMBop" any chance we got. Little did I know that one day at school would be my last day. My mother packed up our family in the middle of the night and we moved away a few towns over to a safe house for abused women. I thought I would never see my friends again.

We lived in the safe house for about two weeks and then moved to another new town, where I lived for the next seventeen years of my life. The school I attended was small, and it fed into a single high school in the city. One day, on the bus to school, I met a brunette named Ashley, who lived one street over from me. It turned out we were in the same class. She was creative, loved music, and was extremely funny. My heart was broken when she told me she was moving and would have to go to a different school. It devastated me, thinking we wouldn't see each other anymore after what I had experienced when I abruptly had to leave my first home.

I had to deal with the sadness of not seeing Ashley for the rest of my elementary days. But then, as a freshman, I was walking the halls one day, and a small, red-haired girl with freckles approached me. She yelled, "Maggie?? Is that really you?"

Confused, I replied, "Yes?"

She took a closer look at me and said "You look the same as you did in first grade! It's ME! Stephanie, from Mrs. Hemphill's class!"

I nearly passed out from excitement! How had *this* happened? I'd never thought I would see Stephanie again. She then continued to tell me that her family had moved away from the town where we'd met and moved right onto the corner of 10th Street . . . right down the hill from the elementary school I'd attended in my third town. I asked, "You mean 10th Street where it runs into Circle Drive?"

She exclaimed, "Yep. My house is the white house with red shutters."

Turns out I had passed her house every single time I left my house for what was probably five years, and we never crossed paths once. Not at the grocery store, not a restaurant (and there were only a handful in the whole town), not at sporting events between our two schools. We'd stayed connected even though we'd thought we might never see each other again: in fact, not only did we stay connected, we'd moved to the *same town*. What are the odds? I'll tell you, it wasn't likely!

But wait, it gets even more connected than we both realize. As we began talking, another freshman walked up to us. Stephanie immediately introduced her as her best friend. . . . But this person looked oddly familiar to me. And then it clicked. It. Was. ASHLEY! Ashley had moved to the same school and had become fast friends with Stephanie. This kind of connection is an expression of how our friendship never separated, even though we were all taken to different places.

When you live the Law of Oneness, you never know who you will see again—and who those people will meet along the way! Stephanie, Ashley, and I spent the next four years as incredibly close friends. This was the first time I truly felt the Law of Oneness and realized we are all connected by something beyond our physical existence.

This law is about the power of connection, and that extends to real-world manifestations of "what goes around comes around." When you live by this law, you are more aware of your thoughts and actions, which also means you tend to be more aligned with other aspects of the universe: things just seem to work out for you, the job you want just lines itself up, suddenly that new puppy you wanted is yours, and maybe your mother-in-law actually apologizes . . . these are all vibrations that are energy. Energy cannot be created or destroyed, so the energy that we tap into when we have a thought is energy that's already in existence. That energy's sole purpose is to fulfill its intention. To exist forever. This principle will be a daily reminder that what happens to one happens to all. When the pain, love, fear, and ecstasy are experienced by one being on this planet, the collective is also a part of that.

Therefore, it's important to approach anything and everything with the understanding that things may not be as they initially seem, but they are always connected.

Application of the Law of Oneness

Journal Prompt: Can you think of a time when you met or coincidentally ran into someone, and this blew your mind?

Daily Gratitude: Reflect on today's blessings. "I embrace connection, I cultivate compassion, and I find gratitude within."

Daily Reflection: If you didn't feel gratitude, journal on why you didn't feel gratitude today. If you felt separation or scarcity, lean into that feeling. What was holding you back from feeling gratitude?

The Law of Vibration

Everything, everything, everything has its own vibration and frequency. The words on this page, the actual page itself, the binding in the book, the audio you're hearing from your phone, you, your clothes, your jewelry, everything. This does not only apply to physical things you can see but also to the nonphysical things: thoughts, feelings, and desires all have a unique vibration of their own.

Gases and liquids have a higher frequency than solids. Think of gases as the emotions of joy, love, and gratitude: they float higher in frequency than the more solid emotions of fear/anger, despair, and grief, which are lower frequencies. When you enter a room, if it has ever felt heavy or light, you've experienced the Law of Vibration. Since the Law of Oneness taught us that we are all beings living on the same organism, we know from the Law of Oneness that we can sense and intuitively feel when something is out of balance with another's energy.

Note that if you are experiencing fear or anger or despair or grief, you are not inherently "low-vibe." Those of us who battle depression or social anxiety, who are grieving, or who are otherwise experiencing difficult emotions are valid, our thoughts are valid, and it is understandable and acceptable to struggle. We can find ways to be grateful and to have compassion and kindness even though we are experiencing hardship. Everyone is on this journey together, and we are all learning how to operate in this world.

Now here's the hard pill to swallow. Your emotions and your energy are bonded with every experience, place, and person you know in your reality. Those things have shaped you into the vibration that you are today.

Some of those bonds are addictions. And those addictions prevent you from bringing new vibrations into your life. You may be addicted to judgment, addicted to anger, addicted to grief and despair—which means that you can't leave any room in your life for creative energy to come in and establish something new. When your vibration is in these lower frequencies, it is almost impossible to welcome this energy that is so essential to remaining connected and expansive. Similarly to a radio station, you have to be on a certain frequency for the music to come through and not be static. You can't be on the AM frequency and expect to hear the FM stations.

Look at the figures on the left side of the diagram on page 24. It illustrates how two atoms bond to make a molecule. This is the common structure that we were all taught in science in middle school. When two atoms get close to each other, they can become bonded, during which the two share information. When two people share an experience of anger, this low frequency bonds them. It has made them connected energetically, because, like the atoms, they are sharing information. Once we share energy and information, it takes more energy to separate. And when you're in a situation in which low-energy vibrations are being shared, the energy that got you into that situation is not the energy that's going to get you out. The Law of Vibration reminds us to investigate how much energy we are using in our interactions, and what kind. It asks us how much of our vibration is being used in these lower frequencies. Once you notice these lower frequencies and you consciously devote the energy that is your creative force to those higher-vibration emotions, you can create a new outer reality.

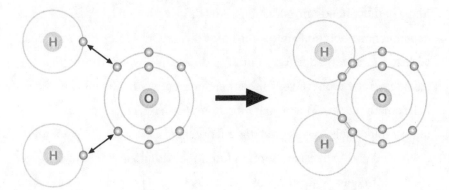

Have you ever just been thinking about someone and you're wondering what they're doing, and they call you on the phone? This is the principle of the Law of Vibration in active motion. Your thoughts are like radio signals, and different stations—in other words, people—can pick up the frequencies that you're sending out.

You are connected to different people throughout your life by different energetic emotions. Energetic emotion is literally energy that is in motion. And when you think of these people, you emit a chemical response from your brain. Working with the principles of this law means prompting yourself to question your emotional addictions. How do you spend your day? If you spend your time judging others, competing with them, gossiping, feeling guilty about who knows what—realize that the thoughts you're thinking are emitting outward into the world around you.

Application of the Law of Vibration

Journal Prompt: Write each negative or low-frequency emotion that you feel throughout the day. Beside each negative or low frequency, add one thing that you are grateful for.

Daily Gratitude: Just for today, I will not allow lower frequencies to inhibit my day. (Add extra gratitude if you are experiencing hardship.)

Daily Reflection: Am I aware of my negative thoughts? How do I feel when they arise? How can I meet them with high-vibration energy?

Law of Correspondence

As Esther Hicks, channeling the messages of Abraham, wrote, "A belief is a thought you keep thinking. A belief is a thought you continue to think. A belief is a thought you continue to repeat in your head and therefore act out with your body." This is a perfect encapsulation of this law.

We often correlate this principle with the phrase "as above, so below" or "as within, so without," both phrases from the ancient Hermetic text *The Emerald Tablet*. Popularized by occultists like Helena P. Blavatsky and William Atkinson, it's meant to illustrate the concept that the inner thoughts and workings of the mind influence the outer world, and therefore your experiences within it. In other words, the outer world is not a filter: it's not going to figure out what you're looking for; it can't read your mind, which means it can't project everything that you already believe. Your outer reality is created by the thoughts that you actively think. Those negative thoughts about what your coworker said the other day; the belief that your parents think you're a failure; the assumption that just because someone doesn't like you, they've told other people not to like you, and everyone gives you anxiety because you think they may not like you, either: Isn't that exhausting?

Are you exhausted?

This principle reminds us that every day, it is very important to take care of the inner chaos that is inside you, because if you do not tame it, the outer world will reflect that chaos back to you. When you work with the Law of Correspondence, you realize the necessity of getting very clear on what it is you don't want and what it is you *do* want. Now that you know each law builds on the law preceding it, you'll understand that it is very crucial to work with this principle before you try to move on to the next step, the ever-popular Law of Attraction. Before you even think of manifesting anything, look inside yourself. You can manifest and write down affirmations and mantras all day long, but if you're not seeing the results that you want, it's almost certainly because the chaos or the confusion inside of you, or the belief inside of you, is saying that you really aren't worthy enough to have this thing that you want.

And it may not be your fault that you're not programmed to believe that you're worthy of having the things that you want. The author Dr. Joe Dispenza writes in *Becoming Supernatural* that 95 percent of our thoughts are a subconscious program, meaning that we are conscious of only 5 percent of our own minds. Dispenza goes on to explain that by the time we are in our thirties, we have perpetuated our habits of feeling, responding, and acting for such a long time and so consistently that we have created a version of ourselves that is solely based on memorized thoughts and reflected emotional patterns learned from our parents and in other relationships, as well as unconscious behaviors that we've picked up as a means of survival. These behaviors might get us through situations that our anxiety has come up with, or save us from the pain of perceptions and subconscious beliefs that make us carry fear or shame about something, but they also limit us.

So if we actually want to create something different in the outside world, we first have to take our mind out of our body, which involves changing our entire state of being.

By the time you've reached this point in the book, you should have already identified and recognized the thought vibrations that you emit throughout the day, so you can start changing them. This is absolutely essential in order to get to the next law, as well as to open yourself up to a metaphysical mindset. You have to give yourself the space to let new realities in, to create and become expansive, and to be limitlessly kind to yourself and the rest of the shared experience of this world. Take the time, as you journal about this law, to truly look inside your inner chaos and confront the issues that are overwhelming and exhausting you, preventing you from taking the next step in this metaphysical journey. The reason you are learning about these laws is simple but profound: to empower yourself with the timeless wisdom that has the potential to elevate your consciousness and bring about positive change.

Application of the Law of Correspondence

Journal Prompt: Did I fill my cup today? What does it look like and feel like when I take care of myself first? How is my day different when I calm my inner chaos?

Daily Gratitude: Name the people who are in your support system. Who are your friends, family, lovers, etc., and in what ways do you appreciate them?

Daily Reflection: My community reminds me to fill my own cup so I can be of service to others. How has my community supported me, and in what way can I return the favor?

The Law of Attraction

Get ready—this is almost everyone's favorite part. The Law of Attraction, also known as "the secret," also known as "the teachings of Abraham, also known as Esther Hicks" . . . the list goes on. This law has been so modernized and made so digestible that your grandmother, aunt, cousin, and best friend are probably all familiar with the concept of manifestation.

We have talked about how impossible living this law is if you haven't thoroughly studied and embodied the principles of the three laws that come before it. If you were trying to jump to the Law of Attraction without spending time with the others, and its teachings aren't working for you, that's why. It's also why some people don't believe in manifestation—they don't know about the building blocks or the stepping stones that are necessary if you actually want to manifest something. Manifesting is more than creating a list of things that you want, or making a vision board. Manifesting is understanding our connected world, being conscious of the energy you're emitting, and embodying a change in your inner world so you can see it reflected in your outer world. Manifestations cannot come true if you don't understand that you will attract what you give your time and attention to. The Law of Attraction is simply that.

Usually when we think of the Law of Attraction, we focus on what we don't have and how having that thing would make our life different. As a result, the thought vibrations that come from our attention to the lack thereof keep attracting it. The fact is that you can't invite anything into your world unless you experience your desire emotionally, as we discussed in regard to the previous law. You are bonded to your emotions and the frequencies they emit. The Law of Attraction tells you to see things as you want them, and this helps you understand that you have to put yourself into an emotionally elevated state of mind in order to attract the things that your inner world wants.

If your body and your mind are in an emotionally elevated state, you are emitting a higher frequency. When you emit that higher frequency, you attract similar frequencies. If you're familiar with your Human Design type, you'll understand how it plays a crucial role in your manifestations. While this book won't delve deeply into Human Design, you can find resources in the back to discover your specific manifestation type.

Your brain doesn't differentiate between an experience that you actually have and an experience that you only imagine. That's why it is so important to build upon these other principles before you get to the Law of Attraction.

By mindfully studying each of the laws in succession, you'll gain the ability to create a scenario that your brain won't be able to identify as real or fabricated. This is how people manifest, and how they quantum-collapse. Quantum collapsing occurs after we use all twelve laws of the universe at the same time with each other. The concept of quantum-collapse challenges our classical intuition, because it implies that the very act of observing a quantum system influences its behavior. This implies that by using each of the laws with an astute awareness, and observing them, it will cause your outer world to react. The "collapse" is similar to Tetris: when you arrange the pieces in a particular format, the entire picture appears to "fall into place." Quantum collapsing happens when you apply these laws and then something in your physical world shifts and reacts.

Application of the Law of Attraction

Journal Prompt: Am I obsessed with manifesting something? Does this emotion or feeling feel desperate or authentic?

Daily Gratitude: What prosperity do you already have within your daily life? Focus on the smallest thing first (like this book, your phone, etc.) and then expand out into your home, your life, your community, your state, etc. Create a momentum of gratitude.

Daily Reflection: Am I bringing desperate energy into my manifestations and therefore pushing them away?

What Is Human Design?

Human Design offers two main manifestation categories: specific and nonspecific types. If you're a nonspecific type, you possess the ability to attract desires effortlessly with a general sense and belief that they will come to fruition. For instance, you may simply envision the type of house or job you want, and it manifests without the need for detailed specificity.

On the other hand, specific types require a more precise approach. For successful manifestation, you must create an elevated state of being and a state of mind, shifting your frequency to align with your desired outcome. Detailed visualization and specificity become crucial in this process.

The Law of Inspired Action

This law is a companion to the Law of Attraction, because it tells you that in order to achieve what you want to attract, you will have to take some kind of physical action. Now, that physical action doesn't have to be something strenuous or elaborate, but there does need to be some kind of movement on your part. And this movement can't be just anything—after all, it's *inspired* action. Uninspired action is the last thing you want to be using to create your manifestations and to achieve a new reality. Inspired action is intentional physicality, which creates an elevated emotion of joy within your body and your being.

Inspired action is more than just creating a vision board. Inspired action means that you take that vision board and you put it beside your bed—or even under your pillow—while you sleep, and then you look at it every morning. You read every single part of it, and you remember the emotion that you felt when you plucked those images off Pinterest and you printed them out and you put them on a physical board. Inspired action is taking that vision board and turning it into digital wallpaper for your phone, so that every time you are checking it, you'll see the subconscious symbolism that you have consciously put on your phone so that you inspire yourself with every action you take.

Even reading this book is an act of inspired action—but the *significant* change (how will you be different in your daily actions? will you be on autopilot or will you be in control? how will you apply the laws?) will be how you use this book for yourself. Reading the words on these pages is just the first step. Putting the ideas you've learned into motion and moving out of your comfort zone—asking yourself the hard questions—will be the inspired action.

Studying metaphysics has taught me one thing, and that is that it's not all sunshine, rainbows, flowers, and kittens. It's real, it's hard, and it's a process of growth. Getting to a metaphysical mindset involves taking real physical action to create the reality that you want. That can mean interacting with the limitations of capitalism in order to get what you need to take the next step. It can mean interfacing with technology—which can be a double-edged sword, given that it can sometimes drain us and cause unnecessary separation. The fact is, we live in a world that is physical but has aspects that are metaphysical, which means we need to learn how to survive in this physical plane. And ultimately, the best way to interact with your environment and put the Law of Inspired Action into effect is not only to use what you have for the greatest good, but also to learn how to use the resources we have for the benefit of all.

Application of the Law of Inspired Action

Journal Prompt: What will you do today to take inspired action? How will you create momentum for the things that you want to come back to you?

Daily Gratitude: What things that would be materialistic do you have that you are very grateful for? Do you feel shame for wanting materialistic items?

Daily Reflection: Where does the emotional charge come from when you take inspired action? Do you feel it in your body?

Law of Perpetual Transmutation of Energy

This one's a mouthful, right? This principle means that once energy moves, that movement is perpetual. It's right there in the name: energy is constantly transmuting itself.

Let's say you have the thought that you want to get up and start working out tomorrow. Simply having the thought creates a transmutation of the energy. And because you're building off the other laws that you have learned, you're defining in very clear terms what you want and what you're going to do to take inspired action in order to transmute that energy.

Stay with me now. How many of you expected to read the first few laws and start seeing instant changes? You magnetized an energy of expectation. And the bad news is that that energy doesn't just fade away—it stays in existence forever. It's existed forever; energy cannot be created or destroyed, meaning it just *is*.

Water is a great example of a perpetual transmutation of energy. Water is a liquid that can transform into a solid or a gas form, but it never goes away completely. When water doesn't physically exist, its energy of the water takes a unique form. We cannot get rid of the energy of water. When water is in a gaseous state (water vapor), it possesses energy in the form of its molecular motion. The water molecules move more freely and at higher speeds compared to when it is in its liquid state. This is an example of the water's energy taking a unique form.

Change is the only constant. With that in mind, let's focus on how you can create a momentum that benefits you by changing the energetic emotional charge in your thoughts. How many times have you experienced a situation where you wanted to just give in to the confusion or anger? Wouldn't it have been amazing if you could transmute that energy and use it to propel your manifestations forward instead?

Energy is always in motion—you just need a steering wheel to guide it. In some situations, you might have grabbed the steering wheel before you even realized that you were driving the car! For example, let's say someone went on social media and blasted their opinion about you, and they were very harsh. You were hurt. They don't even know you, they didn't even try to reach out to you, and they just spread these lies and hate and sent this hateful energy toward you. You saw all this energy being fed toward this person's low vibration of fear, and instead of just reacting, you used this principle to transmute that energy into something else—something productive. So take that energy and transmute it into power and grace while you work out at the gym.

We can transmute the lower vibrations of fear and guilt, anger, and grief into something else, and it doesn't have to happen overnight. Another example: turn your grief into a song that helps you deal with the pain and trauma you've experienced. I once knew a friend who got a mean text from someone and turned it into a song. It was his way of transmuting the energy and hatefulness that he felt from receiving angry words from someone who didn't truly know him anyway. Instead of letting that momentum and energy fester and stew in that lower vibration and then also taking inspired action from those lower vibrations, which is what many people do, he channeled that energy into creativity, and out of it came something truly beautiful.

If you want to see a great example of the Law of Perpetual Transmutation of Energy, look at Taylor Swift's "All Too Well" (the ten-minute version). The creativity and inspiration behind this song led to Taylor transmuting energy from something very heartbreaking and traumatic into something that benefited millions of people. There are so many more examples I could give to showcase how lower energies can be turned into something that creates a higher frequency—but just look toward your favorite artists and you'll see this law in action.

Application of the Law of Perpetual Transmutation of Energy

Journal Prompt: Transmute a traumatic experience into something that is fueled by your creative pursuits. What does that look like for you? Is it a painting, a ten-minute ballad, a movie, a podcast? Use the space in your journal to transmute negative energy with your hands.

Daily Gratitude: Find gratitude in lessons from people who betrayed you in the past. Do I see my lessons as blessings, now that I have transmuted through them?

Daily Reflection: You can always go back to a time that was difficult and be the person you needed in that moment.

Law of Cause and Effect

This principle is pretty cut-and-dry; it can be summed up in the phrase "what goes around comes around." If you intentionally hurt someone, you cause an effect. We're moving away from this old Newtonian thinking that there is a cause and there is an effect when the quantum model and concept continually show us that we can cause the effect. In the quantum world, particles can exhibit behaviors such as entanglement, where the state of one particle is instantly correlated with the state of another, regardless of distance. This non-local behavior is not explained by classical cause-and-effect relationships. The quantum model allows for the concept of causation to be viewed differently. Instead of a straightforward cause leading to a predictable effect, quantum mechanics allows for the notion of causation as a process of influencing or interacting with potential outcomes. The act of observation or measurement itself can influence the behavior of particles and determine their outcomes, highlighting the role of the observer in the process. Let's go into this a little deeper.

This principle gives us the ability to take ownership over our lives and to have a sense of accountability—to know that we have caused some (but not all) of the things that have happened to us.

One of the favorite things that I ever heard from my dear friend Chantal was the phrase "no judgment, no expectation." She reminded me that the universe is neutral, and that it responds to our intentions. You can look back on a situation and think that you did something bad, and you are a bad person, and that caused you to have a terrible effect. But the universe doesn't see it like that. There is no good and bad—there is just what there is. So the universe is not making a judgment about who you are in that situation: it is just responding to how you feel about yourself. If you want to cause an effect in your life, you have to internalize a positive perception of yourself. Do you feel worthy, rich, loved? Or do you feel desperate, shameful, and full of regret?

I am not saying that people who are poor, or struggling, or in adverse situations are having those experiences as a result of their thoughts. What I am saying is that these laws work how they work, and it doesn't matter if we think they are fair or unfair or right or wrong, because they are impartial. Quantum physics tells us that there are both a macrocosm and a microcosm at play. The world, with the reality we correspond with daily, is a very well-developed structure. It is physical, and it is real for all of us. We cannot control what happens on the global scale, the macrocosm, but we can control what is happening in our daily lives and our reality, which is the micro-cosm. When we are causing an effect in the microcosm, as we learned earlier about atoms, it creates bonds with other atoms that also lead into causing an effect. This is when you fully accept, and become empowered by, the realization that your experiences are happening *for* you, not *to* you.

Application of the Law of Karma

Journal Prompt: Write out your top three karmic connections and create a new potential future outcome. A karmic connection is a bond between you and someone else that carries through lifetimes. Sometimes this is between parents, siblings, and other prominent figures in your life. If your relationship dynamic plays out a certain way with your mother or father, perhaps you have a karmic connection to them in another life. How does this apply to you? What connections do you feel have strong karmic bonds?

Daily Gratitude: How can I be grateful to those who may have hurt me in the past? Can I see this situation in a new light?

Daily Reflection: Each person has a "higher self" that isn't always the one in charge. Your higher self can communicate with someone else's higher self (ask permission, of course) to find the clarity or integration needed for you to move through the energy. Can I communicate with my higher self to reflect on past experiences?

Law of Compensation

This law is an extension of the Law of Karma—in the previous law, we learned that "what goes around comes around." In this one, it's a little like the threat you might have received as a kid: "Stop crying, or I'll give you something to cry about!" But instead it's "Be grateful, and I'll give you something to be grateful about"!

The Law of Compensation teaches us that if you focus on certain kinds of thoughts, you will be compensated with more of the same. So if you are constantly thinking about how life is stressful, you never have enough money, you're overworked and underappreciated, and your coworkers are horrible, you are constantly emitting certain thought vibrations, which create neurological pathways.

The mind is the brain in action. So when your mind is using these pathways to navigate stressful situations, they become more concrete—in other words, "what fires together, wires together." There are actually multiple minds in your brain. You use a specific (and different) mind when you meditate, when you draft a spreadsheet, when you make dinner, when you commute. For each type of mind, you create a sequence of neurological networks that work together. These are referred to as neural nets, clusters of neurons that work together. Think of your mind as a smartphone outfitted with multiple apps, each capable of handling a different kind of thought: one for things that you are grateful for, one for the things that bring you joy, and another for those that provide you with comfort. Each time you make the conscious choice to focus on a different kind of thought, the app begins to run; and as it interfaces with your mind, it causes new neurons to fire. New neural pathways begin forming—and those new pathways can create massive changes in your life. In other words, when you consciously create a new kind of mind, the universe has no choice but to respond, creating new neural nets that in turn will re-form your brain and initiate new realities.

If you create thoughts in your mind that bring you down, the universe will continue to bring those things to you. As hard as it might be to hear, your physical reality is a direct experience of the neurological programs you continue to use, as well as the actions you take because of your beliefs. A belief is a thought that you continue to think, which may have its genesis in the beliefs of others—societal programming that existed a long time before you were born and has shaped your brain ever since. The more you repeat the belief, the more your inner reality will become your outer reality.

Application of the Law of Compensation

Journal Prompt: What are the five thoughts I think the most every day? What vibration frequency am I on with these thoughts?

Daily Gratitude: Remember that although you can change your mindset this moment, that doesn't mean your entire "hard drive" is going to update overnight. It takes time, but the sheer awareness that you want to think on a different wavelength is the momentum that can propel you up.

Daily Reflection: Do you enjoy being in a state of anxiety or tension? What happens when you allow yourself to relax? What comes up for you?

Law of Relativity

The Law of Relativity tells us that nothing is good or bad—it just *is*. You don't have to love your experiences. You don't have to hate your experiences. It is your perception that creates these judgments. This law suggests that the challenges you face in life are part of a bigger picture as you become your most developed self. Later in this book, we will get into the Akashic records, including the theory that our higher selves choose the challenges that we will have in our Earthly incarnation to develop. But for now, let's dive in to the lessons of this law.

Now, when I tell you to view something from a neutral place, that doesn't mean you have to allow someone to evade accountability. Viewing things from a place of neutrality is a great way to realize that there are multiple perspectives to every experience in life. For example, in this day and age of social media, it's hard not to compare your life to other people you see when you're scrolling through your feed. The Law of Relativity reminds you that comparison is the biggest source of disappointment—it extinguishes joy. You can never be sure of what is happening in someone else's life, so the need to compare the differences between you and your neighbor inhibits you from creating change that you see as an imbalance.

You may see your neighbor as being in a better position because he has a nicer lawn, a nicer car, a bigger porch . . . whatever it may be, it's all relative. The Law of Relativity teaches us not to compare our problems to someone else's, because we do not really know what is going on in that person's life; in reality they could be in a far worse situation than ours. This law suggests that because we are inclined to compare everything, nothing has meaning until we assign it meaning.

When you compare someone, you are creating a void that is impossible to fill, because you have bred an expectation that is unrealistic.

Applying this law to your daily life can be very difficult if you have trouble seeking forgiveness for the people who cast judgment on you throughout your life. But with practice and your knowledge of the other laws, you'll begin to understand that holding on to the negative thoughts of those who have judged you only brings more judgment into your life. When you can look at your thoughts from a neutral state and consciously create new neural pathways, you will become free from your cycles of negative thought and subconscious programming—instead of a single cluster of programmed experiences, you will be welcoming in a community of new experiences, new neural creations that will work *with* the quantum aspects of the universe instead of against them.

As Eckhart Tolle put it in his book *A New Earth*, "In form, you are and will always be inferior to some, superior to others. You are neither inferior nor superior to anyone. True self-esteem and genuine humility arise out of that realization. In the eyes of the ego, self-esteem and humility are contradictory. They are the same."

Application of the Law of Relativity

Journal Prompt: Do you believe in forgiveness? Can forgiveness look like forgiving the self without forgiving the other? What does forgiveness look like to me?

Daily Gratitude: Think on a time when you were the one who needed the grace of forgiveness. How did this feel, and how does this help you with what you know now?

Daily Reflection: Is there a time when you have seen the Law of Relativity play out before your eyes? Can you move forward from a neutral state of mind, knowing their higher self knows better?

Law of Polarity

This principle tells us that although things may seem opposite, they are two inseparable parts of the same thing. The key is integrating these changes into your life so that you do not experience immense burnout. It is important to remain aware of the intensity of your meditation practice, workout routine, productivity, and creativity every single day—the key to remaining balanced. Certain weather patterns don't last: they come and go in cycles. We also ebb and flow as the cycles of Earth. Don't be afraid to embrace change.

I remember the first month of 2023 in California, when it seemed to rain every single day, which was uncommon. Everyone in Los Angeles was losing their mind because this change was so drastic, but then the springtime came. The extreme rains and the shifting seasons caused a superbloom, a rare phenomenon in which so many flowers grew that they could be seen from space. Everyone appreciated the beauty that came out of that challenging time. When we think about this event in the context of this law, we can remember that although we go through really hard times, we're being set up for something far greater. It's how we integrate those challenges and work with the things that come up for us in life that can lead to transformative experiences.

Our challenges are stepping stones to our greatest accomplishments. I wouldn't have had the strength to write this book if I hadn't been through emotional abuse. That was the hardest time in my life so far, and I am grateful for the challenges that I overcame and the battles that I won after that. Dealing with the grief of having someone who I trusted turn on me in the cruelest way possible, using the justice system as a white person against a Black woman, is an extreme polarity that I never thought I would experience.

Working with this principle means understanding that challenges will happen, and it's how we integrate those challenges and deal with them that will provide us with more of what we are looking for. In this context, "integrate" refers to the process of assimilating, incorporating, or embracing the challenges that arise in our lives. Sometimes putting yourself in someone else's shoes is a great way to see the polarity of our current situation.

Application of the Law of Polarity

Journal Prompt: What's something that happened to me that I saw as a failure but was a lesson for success?

Daily Gratitude: Can I put myself in someone's shoes who wishes they had what I had?

Daily Reflection: What challenges will I overcome today?

Law of Rhythm (also called Law of Perpetual Motion)

I know you may not want to do this, but I want you to look back on the hardest experiences in your life and see how they propelled you. The Law of Rhythm builds on the Law of Polarity, highlighting the fact that although you might go through something that's hard, it will not last forever. The same principle applies to those of you who are constantly waiting for the other shoe to drop: the seasons change, beliefs change, individual people change society—changes bring more changes, because everything is always in perpetual motion.

It's important to know that everyone's rhythm is different. Sometimes things happen for other people faster than they happen for you. That doesn't mean that the universe is working for them and against you—it means that all people are moving at their own pace. The body's aging process is a great real-world example of the Law of Rhythm. Although some people make an attempt at putting the aging process in reverse with Botox and fillers and skin-tightening treatments, the aging process still happens eventually. Our physical bodies are in states of constant change, and there's no way to truly put a stop to, or reverse, the perpetual motion of time.

This principle also reminds us to continue to see the good in things. There's always a potential for new momentum, new programming, or a different frequency, even if it seems like you're trapped in a negative situation. In order to change, the first thing you should do is try to listen to the rhythm of your daily life. For example, maybe you're the kind of person who needs more sleep than others, but you force yourself to stay awake for productivity's sake. This constant battling with your own rhythm will create a change that you dislike—it's up to you to respect your own pace and create a life that will support it. That is the only way to change your frequencies, create new thoughts and neural pathways, and therefore support new, more positive realities.

It's okay to acknowledge the negative things that will come up in life, but it is also important to cherish the blissful times and have gratitude for the way things are constantly in motion. Remember, just because things are going great doesn't mean that the scales can't tip. Everything in the universe has patterns and rhythms and cycles. Be mindful and try not to be so hard on yourself for making what seemed to be bad choices.

Application of the Law of Rhythm

Journal Prompt: What's your "polar opposite"?

Daily Gratitude: What are things you have now that you never believed you would have?

Daily Reflection: At one point you were on the complete opposite side of something you wanted. You made a goal, and you reached it. You are in a constant state of growth. Do you have doubts in your ability to keep achieving your goals? Why?

Law of Balance (also called the Law of Gender)

This law deals with the energy that is available in the universe. These are often referred to as the yin and yang, or the masculine and feminine. However, in this instance the terms "masculine" and "feminine" are not defined by gender or sex. They each represent different properties in our life, and it is essential that they remain balanced. It is not beneficial to have a surplus of yin energy or yang energy. Rather, these energies should coexist with each other so that the conscious and the subconscious mind work together effectively. This is the last law of the Laws of the Universe, and the one that ties them all together. Imagine this law as the scales of justice: on one scale, you have energy that is giving, receiving, being compassionate, and expressing emotion. On the other scale you have an energy that is action-oriented, is ready to resolve the problem, is determined, and is closely aligned with the conscious mind.

It is essential to have balance within these energies, just like it's essential for the seed to be pollinated. We cannot have one without the other: there cannot be an excess of yin energy without having a negative imbalance of the yang energy. This means that in any situation, it is important to try to pull from both energies of the yin and the yang, the masculine and feminine, to achieve the solution to a problem. When you can find a way to embody equal amounts, you will have mastered this law.

To learn how to balance these energies, we must know more about each one. This is a constant growth and learning process, but here is what we can break down from the two energies and how they exhibit themselves in the world:

Masculine energy: Based on learned knowledge, it is logic, stability, risk management, drive, and goals. If you are the person who people come to when they have a problem that needs to be solved, or when they need someone to be in control, you are probably a masculine-dominant-energy type of individual.

Feminine energy: Based in a "knowing," it is creativity, clairvoyance, intuition, understanding, compassion, and openness. If you are someone that people come to when they need advice, or when they need an intuitive perspective or want empathy, you are probably a feminine-dominant-energy type of individual.

Creating a balance of these energies doesn't mean that if you spend all day working on something and taking action, you must receive or do something creative that same day, too. When you use your intuitive abilities to make decisions based on which change or integration is going to be best for you, this is a utilization of your feminine energies. If you're taking action-oriented steps toward your goals, you're leaning into your masculine energy. You will have to use both kinds of energies throughout your life, but self-awareness about which energy you are leaning into at any given moment is the catalyst for becoming more balanced. When you are overly reliant on masculine or feminine energy, you may begin to see signs of burnout.

For some people, it's going to be really hard to sit in this feminine energy, because you've been relying on masculine energy for such a long time. Just being with yourself, feeling your emotions, and working through each of these laws will help you maintain a balance of energy in your everyday life. Once you are more balanced in your energy output and input, you will begin to see things from a perspective that is beyond the physical.

Application of the Law of Balance

Journal Prompt: What does balancing energy look like to me? What's something I've never considered doing because it doesn't fit in the proverbial box?

Daily Gratitude: Where do I have balance in my life?

Daily Reflection: Wake up and for one day try to live and apply every law that resonates with you the most that day. Keep your journal under your pillow when you sleep.

MEDITATION FOR THE LAWS OF THE UNIVERSE

Find a comfortable place to sit. Close your eyes and inhale slowly for four seconds, holding the breath for four seconds, then exhaling for four seconds. Do this for one minute.

Now imagine you are standing at the base of a tree. You realize that there is an entryway in the trunk. Through this portal are two staircases that descend to the right and left, as well as a path that enables you to walk straight through. Pick your path and then start creating your own. As you follow it, you are taking ten steps. That can be any way you choose: walking up or down stairs, forward toward a hallway of doors, straight into a forest, etc.

Begin to take those steps. *Ten.* You're aware of your breath. *Nine.* You are aware of each footfall. *Eight.* You see something manifesting in front of you. *Seven.* It is the guide you have been looking for. But everything is still very much out of focus. So you take another deep breath. *Six.* You can see the end of the staircase, and there is another door. *Five.* Colors and other symbolism show up for you around the door. *Four.* You are just a few steps away from grabbing the handle. Visualize what the handle looks like to you. *Three.* Feel gratitude for being on this path and what you are about to be shown. *Two.* Take another deep breath and exhale to express your relief. *One.* Open the door. Stay in this space for as long as you like. Ask a question or hold an intention. When you are ready to leave, walk back the way you came, out of the tree trunk.

When you arise from this meditation, you are walking into the day as your new self—the self that knows the laws of the universe and knows how to use them. You are going to be the most intentional, conscious version of yourself, starting now.

CHAPTER 4

THE BRAIN IS YOUR BEST MANIFESTING FRIEND

In this chapter we're specifically going to talk about how the brain can be used for manifesting. Because we've learned about all twelve universal laws, not only the Law of Attraction, we should have a more nuanced view of what it takes to cocreate the realities you wish to see in this world. We're in the right mental space; we understand the work that we must do. But first let's talk more about how the brain works. If you're ready to do a deep dive into the inner workings of neural pathways, vibrations, emotions, and how your understanding of their interaction can get you to your desired outcome, grab a cup of tea, because this chapter is going to take you for a ride.

Every time you feel an emotion or you have a thought, you are creating a biochemical reaction that begins in your brain and releases a certain chemical signal. Put very simply, this is how the ethereal becomes physical. An immaterial thought exists before it becomes matter because of the chemical signals. The chemical signals in your body from your brain make your body feel exactly what you are thinking about. This works with the Law of Perpetual Motion: as you create this momentum and energy inside your brain, you continue to admit these chemical signals to your body, which will generate more of that feeling. For example, you just thought of something incredibly stressful and then you felt anxiety. The moment you feel this stress, that emotion creates momentum, and this creates even more stress. Think of it like an avalanche: it's just going to gain momentum until it runs its course.

As Dr. Joe Dispenza writes in his book *Becoming Supernatural*, "If thoughts are the vocabulary of the brain and feelings are the vocabulary of the body, and the cycle of how you think and feel becomes your state of being, then your entire state of being is in the past." Think of yourself as a computer that has been running the same program for decades. If you haven't upgraded your beliefs and your thought patterns, you're essentially running on Windows 98 or MacOS 10 when you should have moved on to a new operating system many, many times over. When you constantly think the same thoughts, believe the same beliefs, and allow yourself to perpetuate the same mental patterns, you are conditioning your body to adhere to this old program. Then you wonder why you can't manifest change. But if you continue to make the same old choices, you will make the neurological networks in your brain even more concrete. Thinking about the things that went wrong in the past instead of creating and building the future that you want within your manifestations will not help you achieve your goals. To create your tomorrow, you must stop thinking about yesterday.

Manifesting is creating from the unknown. If you are fearful or have anxiety about the future, you will never break out of the habits that continue to inhibit your growth. If you stay comfortable in your usual

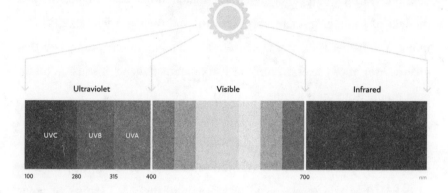

The Spectrum of Light

routines—waking up looking at your email, scrolling through Instagram and TikTok constantly, repeatedly checking your texts to see if you got a response from someone—you aren't giving yourself any space for something new to come in. Stop and ask yourself why you're doing what you're doing and thinking what you're thinking.

Stop thinking about that person who Did You Wrong a year ago or two years ago or ten years ago. Forget that they existed, and move on. Your future will be better and your brain will be healthier if you do.

Our bodies produce a measurable electromagnetic field that surrounds us. It is always emitting light energy, frequencies that carry a specific message or intention. Humans can't even see all the spectrums of light: we cannot see radio waves, we cannot see microwaves;

we can only see a small spectrum of light frequency, as described in the graph to the left.

Our electromagnetic field attracts energy that is reminiscent of the experiences that we have already had. The only way that we can manifest a change in our life is to create a space for energy that is aligned to what we *haven't* already experienced. If you look in the mirror and tell yourself you're a millionaire and you don't feel like this is going to be your reality, you are not magnetizing your manifestation to you—you are only magnetizing the doubt that you are not worthy enough to have the manifestation. But how do you eliminate doubt and maintain space for your manifestation? You are creating discord within yourself, and the outer world will reflect that back to you.

A Harvard study took place with a group of volunteers who had never played the piano. First, researchers split the group into two. Half of the group practiced for two hours a day over the course of five days. Instead of physically moving their fingers, the other half just imagined that they were sitting in front of the piano. The researchers then did brain scans, which showed that both groups had a dramatic number of new neural circuits and programming near their brains that controls the movements of their fingers, even though one group never actually laid hands on the piano. This means that when you mentally rehearse actions that your brain has not already experienced, it can think they have already happened. When you continually fire and wire different brain circuits together with manifestations that you want, the more you practice the manifestation— or run that program in your mind—the easier it will be to manifest.

Another study from the Cleveland Clinic investigated ten researchers between the ages of twenty and thirty-five. One group imagined that they were flexing one of their biceps as hard as they could during five training sessions that lasted over twelve weeks. The other group actually did the muscle flexing. On even-numbered weeks, the researchers recorded the subject's brain activity during the sessions, then measured the strength of the muscle. By the end of the study, even the subjects that had not actually used their muscles at all had increased their bicep's strength by over thirteen percent, and they even maintained that gain after the training sessions stopped. This is proof that your mind is more powerful than you give it credit for.

Our thoughts and emotions play a significant role in shaping our physical and mental well-being. When we experience emotional reactions to situations, they trigger genes in our cells to either activate or deactivate. These genes influence the production of proteins, which are essential for the functioning and structure of our body.

If we consistently experience negative emotions like stress and anxiety, our genes may be downregulated, leading to health issues and limiting our body's ability to function optimally. This can even lead to the expression of genetic diseases that run in families.

Changing our emotions is crucial, because it alters the signals we send to our DNA, resulting in the production of different proteins. This, in turn, affects our physical and mental health. Even if we change our external environment, if we continue to hold on to negative emotions our body becomes addicted to them, and we will keep creating the same experiences.

Our brain has neural networks that form pathways based on our thoughts and experiences. The more we repeat certain thoughts and emotions, the more automatic these pathways become. We have networks for various aspects of our life, such as relationships, work, health, and more.

To manifest something new in our lives, we must pay attention to the energies we are holding on to. Letting go of negative emotions and focusing on positive ones helps us create higher vibrational frequencies. Our thoughts and emotions shape our reality, so it's essential to break free from negative addictions and create a balanced and positive mindset to attract the experiences we desire.

If you're exhausted by focusing your attention on negative emotions—gossip, defensiveness, being stressed—you won't have any energy left to put into your manifestations. You cannot manifest under stress. No matter how many podcasts you listen to or how many people tell you it's totally okay, it is nearly impossible to manifest what you want if you are manifesting from stress.

Turning Away from Fight-or-Flight

When you are stressed and you have intense anxiety, your body is emitting a chemical called cortisol that creates enormous amounts of energy in response to whatever you are stressed about. This has its roots in a primordial response often called "fight-or-flight" that enabled us to survive in our earliest incarnations as human beings, when we were constantly threatened by predators and other environmental stressors. In our modern lives, we don't have to stay in fight-or-flight mode to survive.

But sometimes everyday stresses can trigger it: to our brains, which are still wired for prehistoric dangers, an email or text is just as likely as a saber-toothed tiger to send us into a spiral of downward emotions. The fight-or-flight response creates the feeling that you are being chased or that something is otherwise threatening your life, even if the only threat present is a particularly nasty message from your boss.

When you're in a situation where your body is reacting in this way, remember what you learned about the last law of the universe, the Law of Balance. If you are constantly in a state where your cortisol and adrenaline levels are extremely high, you will have zero ability to return yourself to balance. When you feel completely at the mercy of high stress, this creates an unhealthful magnetic frequency that emanates from you like an aura. And as we've learned, this will only continue to attract more of the same. How many times have you been stressed out, focusing on things that create an imbalance in your life, and then things continually seem to go wrong? When you start the day off thinking that things are going to go badly or that you're not wanted, you are creating a neurological network that is damaging to your evolution.

Brain Waves

So how can you change the chemical expression in your brain, creating the right environment in your internal world so that you can manifest something in your outer world? The answer is in brainwave frequencies.

Beta brain waves can be measured as either low-, medium-, or high-range. When you're in the low beta range, you are relaxed. You don't perceive that there are any threats or triggers that you need to be aware of. This is when you are scrolling aimlessly on your phone, waiting for your coffee, or reading a book in your favorite comfy chair.

When you're mid-range, typically you are in a group, or you are being asked to remember someone's name, or you see someone's face and you can't quite remember who they are. You're not on high alert, but you are in more of a vigilant state, giving you a heightened sense of awareness. Mid-range beta can be referred to as good stress.

High-range beta waves are produced when your hormones and cortisol are going crazy. These are the brain waves that you exhibit when you are in survival mode, experiencing emotions like fear, shame, agitation, grief, anger, and even depression. High-range beta waves can be over

Binaural Beats

There are many ways to use external stimuli to help your brain reach an optimal brainwave frequency for manifestations. One way is to tap in to what is called a binaural beat. A study in the late 1970s proposed that when one tone is played in one ear and a different tone is played in the other, the two hemispheres of the brain connect and create a third tone called a binaural beat. Binaural beats synchronize the brain and help provide clarity, alertness, and incredible concentration. There is solid evidence that shows that the brain and the body respond both in a physical and a cognitive way to binaural beats. Binaural beats can be found all over the Internet, and even on playlists on Spotify.

three times higher than low-range beta and twice as high as mid-range beta. This implies that during periods of intense mental concentration and focus, the brain produces significantly higher-frequency beta waves compared to when we are in a relaxed or moderately engaged state.

So, when you are feeling the stressful emotions associated with high-range beta brain waves, it is much harder to bring yourself back to a balanced low range because of how much energy is being expressed in your elevated state.

Alpha brain waves are frequencies that you exhibit when you are being creative or intuitive. When you aren't analyzing everything and you're accepting the outer world as it is, your alpha brain waves show that you are placing attention on your inner self. Alpha brain waves can be formed while you are in meditation, or even when you are just daydreaming.

Whenever you go to sleep, your brain moves into the theta brain frequency. The theta frequency and the delta frequency are both associated with deep meditations and restorative sleep. Theta frequency has been found in some studies of people who are meditating and then move into a deep sleep. If you prefer to meditate lying down, this may have happened to you. This is a signal that you are dipping into your delta frequencies and producing very high amplitudes of energy. The meditation itself doesn't produce the exhaustive feelings; rather, the act of deep meditation can lead the body to rest and the brain to produce a lot of energy.

There are also gamma-frequency brain waves, which are very high frequency and occur when the brain becomes aroused by an internal event. That could be something like meditation where you have an intense realization or sudden moment of clarity. This meditation is keeping the mind in a more active state rather than a restorative state, as opposed to external stimuli in the physical world. To achieve these heightened frequencies of brain waves, you have to put yourself in the present moment while you are meditating. That means not thinking about your boss, not thinking about your problems, not thinking about when your children might come in and interrupt you.

A deep state of meditation is necessary to fire new circuits in your brain—to signal new genes, new emotions, and ultimately a successful manifestation. If you keep doing this, you can break the cycle of creating negative energy—the belief that your manifestations won't come true because they're not true now—and build a new electromagnetic field around your body.

The long and short of it is that you can create change—but to do that, you have to produce a level of energy that is greater than the fear, the jealousy, the shame, the grief—which isn't easy. If you want to have infinite possibilities, you must feel like you are infinite.

So, how do you feel like you are infinite?

Quantum collapsing is a powerful phenomenon where you generate an intensified and elevated state of emotion that has a profound impact on the physical world around you. When you reach this heightened emotional state, the energy you emit becomes so potent that it accelerates the manifestation process, making your desired outcomes materialize more swiftly.

The essence of quantum collapsing lies in tapping into the quantum field, where time is relative and possibilities are boundless. In this realm, there are no constraints of linear time, and manifestations can seemingly arise out of nowhere. When you create a change or manifestation through quantum collapsing, it may feel like your desires come into being effortlessly and unexpectedly.

To achieve this state of quantum collapsing, you must immerse yourself in an elevated emotional frequency, broadening your emotional spectrum to encompass immense positivity and belief. This amplifies your energetic output, creating a resonance that aligns with the frequencies of your desires, drawing them toward you with greater efficiency.

By understanding and harnessing quantum collapsing, you gain the ability to transcend the limitations of conventional cause-and-effect thinking (the opposite of quantum thinking). Instead of waiting for external circumstances to bring about your desired outcomes, you become the catalyst, generating the necessary energy and intention to manifest your dreams rapidly.

Embracing quantum collapsing empowers you to tap into the realm of infinite potential, where time is nonlinear and possibilities are unlimited. It opens the gateway to cocreating your reality with the quantum field, allowing you to manifest your intentions more effectively and experience the wonders of rapid and seemingly magical manifestations.

How to Change Your Reality

There was a French researcher named René Peoc'h who studied the power of the energetic field surrounding living things. He did this with a study of baby chicks. When a chick is born, it imprints, or bonds, to its mother. But if the chick is born and the mother is not there, the chick will bond to the first moving object they see. That could even be a human being, which is why we sometimes see these relationships between people and their chickens that look like something out of a fairy tale—with the chicken following the human around as if they were its mother. Peoc'h intended to test the energy created by this kind of imprinting. He conducted a test in which a computerized robot would turn sporadically, with no determined pattern, moving left and right an equal number of times. He observed that during the study, the robot seemed to cover the floor equally when there were no baby chicks present. But then something interesting happened. After he began exposing the robot to the newly hatched chicks, they bonded to the robot, imprinted on it, and then followed it around as if it were their mother. Then, he separated the chicks and the robot with a divider so that the chicks could see the robot but not get close to it. What happened next will truly blow you away. Are you ready?

The electromagnetic field from the chicks influenced the robot's movements, so that instead of random movements, it remained in the field that was closest to the chicks. The chicks' intentions influenced the movements of the computer.

The connection is obvious: just like the baby chicks influenced the robot's movements through their electromagnetic field and intention, you also possess the power to change your reality. If these tiny creatures can alter the behavior of a computerized robot, imagine the potential with you to create a new future for yourself, starting right now. Your thoughts, emotions, and intentions can shape the course of your life, attracting new potential outcomes. Embrace the understanding that you are not as limited as you believe; you are not limited by your past patterns or programmed responses; you do have the capacity to shape and transcend your reality according to your desires.

Manifesting and Quantum Collapsing

So, what is the quantum field? It is in this space of infinity, which is sometimes called the unified field, where we actively build our manifestations. This is the space where we can be wealthy, or loved, or travel—it's the space where you have the unlimited potential to create. Quantum physics tells us that these possibilities can exist as electromagnetic potentials in this space. The reason that you cannot physically feel these potentials with your senses is because they are ethereal: they are not existent in time and space yet. These potentials are only present as thought vibrations that can enable you to create a manifestation by connecting your energy with your intention.

Think back to the Law of Oneness: you are a part of the unlimited consciousness of everything and everyone within all the possibilities. So when you observe a potential manifestation in the quantum, it's just like becoming aware of your body in the physical world. You are already a part of it—it's already happening. In the same way, the potential for any manifestation already exists. When we align with the energy of that potential, holding space for our intention causes a "quantum collapse" when the fields of energy collapse into particles. This is referred to as a quantum event. When this happens, your intention becomes an experience that you pull into your own particle frequency in the three-dimensional field. When you are putting your body into a state of awareness that the intention you want to come true has already happened, your brain believes that the event has actually taken place. The more "real" it is for you in your mind, the more likely you are to actually create it in the physical world. Remember, the brain doesn't know this event hasn't actually happened. You are programming your body to the future to access the untapped possibilities, rather than a past that's limited.

When you complete the visualization or meditation, however you decided to manifest, you will maintain some sense of joy, gratitude, and appreciation. When you continually retrain your brain and body to do this, in the end you have created a new self biologically, preventing yourself from falling back into your old programming and the lower vibrational frequencies that can keep you stuck in the past.

BRINGING THE ETHEREAL TO PHYSICAL REALM

Thinking about your manifestations will not bring them into physical reality. You must bring inspired action to what you wish to change in your life. Therefore, writing, or another physical activity, is essential. Journaling, in particular, is a perfect quantum-collapsing tool: putting your downloads into a note will help you bring tangible energy to the ideas swirling around in your head. So instead of thinking about an experience you want to bring into your life, this meditation is going to allow you to actively live that experience.

We are going to break your desires down into seven major objectives, listed below. Do not add any time frames—when you project a timeline for your manifestation, you are immediately inhibiting its flow. So get out your specific journal just for this book and begin expressing the manifestations you intend to cocreate!

- Vacations
- Health
- Business/Money
- Home
- Family
- Friendship
- Love Life

Start by finding your physical form of inspired action. Maybe that is journaling, creating a vision board out of magazines, or creating a digital vision board. You will not use these physical tools until the meditation is complete, but you will want them on hand to use immediately afterward.

You can do the following meditation once a day for seven days. Begin by sitting in a comfortable position and closing your eyes. Place your right hand, with your palm down, on your right knee, and your left hand, with your palm up, on your left knee. Your body receives energy through the left side and gives energy through the right side. Imagine that you are sitting on a beautiful cliff in a meadow surrounded by vast open space. You feel the wind on your cheeks, you hear the birds, and the soft and soothing sounds of water flow serenely down a tranquil stream. You are supported by the ground underneath you. You are aware of the massive potential possibilities that exist with you in this space. Starting with your head, notice the scent of your first core aim, whether that be the love of your life, a trusted family member, the location of your next vacation, or the food you will eat once you have a better income.

Immerse yourself in the olfactory experience of your core aim before moving your awareness to your eyes. How does your vacation look? What does it look like when the love of your life is sitting across from you?

Sit in this quantum experience until you feel comfortable in moving your awareness to the back of your throat. What do you say now that you've manifested the love of your life, your dream family, your dream home, your dream job?

Bring your awareness to your heart. How does your heart feel while you are on vacation, now that you've healed yourself, when you've manifested the love of your life and are sitting comfortable beside them?

Move down to your gut and bring an awareness to the knowledge that comes out of the quantum field. Revel in the trusting feeling you experience by knowing exactly what next steps to take. You trust that the thoughts you are sending out will magnetize back to you, exactly as what you've projected. As you breathe into this infinite quantum potential, it's time to take your awareness away from your physical being and open yourself to receive new potential experiences.

Think about how all the things you want can come to you. See yourself emitting a new frequency, a new electromagnetic vibration. See this energy finding this manifestation and attracting it to you. Allow a smile to spread across your face as you experience bliss, love, appreciation, gratitude, and freedom in this place. Surrender your manifestations and allow quantum collapse to happen: the elevated energy is collapsing the particles to bring you what you want.

Get up from your meditation as if what you have asked for in the seven main objectives has already come true. This is not pretending, or faking it until you make it. This is broadcasting a new electromagnetic frequency so that you can actively create a new life.

This will not happen in one meditation. You will need to reprogram your mind from years of running different software. When you begin, your mind will try to do everything it can to prevent you from sitting and staying in this place. Do not allow the program to become the driver!

CHAPTER 5

ETHEREAL REMINDERS

Y ou've studied the laws of the universe and have learned how to reach beyond the limits of time and space in order to accelerate your manifestations. To continue to improve your ability to see beyond the physical and tap into the limitless knowledge you've begun to sense by beginning to work with the quantum field, it's so important to begin to look toward what I'm calling "calling cards" that the universe is always sending, in order to communicate with you and share wisdom.

Understanding and recognizing the significance of these calling cards is intricately connected to our ability to access vital information within the ethereal realm. Just as the concept of understanding these signs involves recognizing the subtle synchronicities—seemingly coincidental events that actually have cosmic significance—that guide us through life, it also lays the groundwork for our intuitive faculties to attune to higher frequencies of consciousness. These calling cards act as gateways, training our minds to be receptive to subtle energies and connections.

Calling cards from the universe show up in thousands of different ways. It's learning how to decipher them that is key. But when you have a greater understanding of these synchronicities, you can recognize and decode them: series of numbers, letters, lyrics, overheard conversations, billboards, the list goes on and on—what might seem inconsequential to an untrained mind can be a source of enlightenment to anyone with a metaphysical mindset.

Let me share a juicy example!

My friend Brett loves Taylor Swift: he has the amazing ability to match any moment in life with a quote from one of her songs, and it's always pitch-perfect. Brett also absolutely lives to find symbolism around him. He will whip his phone out to take a photo of a license plate if it contains a 444, 777, or 999, and is generally very in tune and aware of what his "calling cards" are.

Brett was lucky enough to get opening night tickets to the Eras Tour, which kicked off a series of events full of calling cards from the universe. First, his alarm didn't go off in time the morning of the concert, so he got on the road later than planned and ended up in a thirteen-hour traffic jam caused by a terrible car wreck. However, he realized that if he'd gotten on the road when he originally planned, he would have been at the site of the wreck right as it happened. Eerie.

When Brett realized he might have been in that horrific accident, he immediately felt that he was being guided. He finally made it to his destination, where he joined up with his crew. At the concert, all of them planned to wear a special bracelet for their friend Betty, who was a Swiftie but sadly had died by suicide during the pandemic.

At one point everyone was in the pool talking about what the set list was going to have on it. What songs would she play? Would she play entire albums? Would she only play what she had already re-recorded? Brett mentioned that he hoped she would play the song she wrote for her grandmother where she says the line "If I didn't know better, I'd think you're still around." He said that he didn't think she would ever play such a sad song on tour, but hoped she would anyway because it reminded him of their friend Betty.

After opening night, TikTok was washed out with thousands of videos, but the only one I remember is Brett shaking the camera, wailing happily, while accompanied by the lyrics "What died didn't stay dead." You know when you are so shocked and shaken by the pure realization that you asked for something and it showed up? That's how he felt in the moment.

Weeks later, Brett was in his home in Los Angeles, lying in his bed and battling with his depression. He was quiet, just thinking about everything happening in his life and running through many scenarios in his head—contemplating what he was supposed to be doing with his life. Even though he had just seen his favorite artist in concert on her nationwide tour's opening night, he was feeling sad. He was missing his friend Betty, and his energy was low.

As Brett was lying in his bed, his Alexa started playing a song he had never heard before. He found out the song was from a Christian artist who he was unfamiliar with, Michael Smith. Since it reminded him of Betty, he texted her mother and mentioned it. As it turned out, Betty and her mother used to listen to that exact song! It was about being surrounded by forces invisible to you: support from those who love you.

Then it got even more mind-blowing: Brett took to social media to tell this story, and one of his friends told him that it's actually possible to listen to audio of the prompts that people asked his device. For example, you can get audio of anyone who asks your Alexa to set a timer, report the weather, or play a song. So Brett brought up his account and scrolled down to the moment the song was played. He listened to a few prompts to make sure he believed what his friend told him, and then he saw the prompt: "Play Michael Smith." He listened, and discovered that it wasn't his voice. Instead, it was someone speaking in a high-pitched tone with a sing-song cadence to the way they said "smi-ith." Chills ran down his entire body because it was . . . her . . . voice. It was Betty's voice, clear as day, saying "Play Michael Smith."

"How? What? I'm crying, I'm seriously crying!" he told me in between gasps of trying to catch his breath. He says he knew it was her, and this just confirms it even more. He was filled with a sense of hope, faith, and unconditional love, and just like that . . . he got a text from a television producer asking him to come in to talk about being on a show on a major network. It was Betty who told him he was going to be famous and would use his platform to help those struggling with mental health— it was almost as if she were reminding Brett about his mission and help- ing him from beyond the physical realm. She was letting Brett know, in the most modern way, that he wasn't alone. No matter how alone he felt.

The people you have loved and lost in life are thinking of you, and you may experience signs and synchronicities like Brett did when they reach out to communicate. Nonphysical communication—whether from loved ones or the universe—is part of the metaphysical mindset, and can open your mind up to new possibilities if you can get familiar with this concept.

In ancient civilizations like Mesopotamia, it was commonplace for people to expect to encounter nonphysical spirits. Pliny references ghosts in his writings and spoke of seeing "an old man who was covered in chains haunting him around Athens." Lucian and Plautus wrote about similar phenomena. In 2014, the World History Encyclopedia noted that all major ancient civilizations held beliefs that the soul of the body existed outside of the body after the body died.

Another example I can share with you is one from my own personal experience. In October 2015, after my mother's passing, I was driving my young children to her funeral when a song, "Lean on Me" by Bill Withers, played on the radio. This song held a special memory from my childhood when my mother told us it would always be her song to us, a reminder that she'd be with us no matter what. Strangely, on the day of the funeral, my brother and I, who were miles apart, both heard the same song on different radio stations. It felt like a powerful sign from her.

Years later, on my birthday, while I was with someone I deeply cared for, the same song played on the radio, bringing tears to my eyes. However, as I looked out the window, I saw a field of miniature ponies, and my heart filled with love, reminding me of my mother's paintings. These moments of synchronicity and meaningful signs were like calling cards from my mother, reminding me to remain open to the love that surrounds us.

In the metaphysical mindset, I've come to understand that these signs are not coincidences, but rather meaningful connections between the physical and nonphysical realms. They serve as gentle reminders to

Real Calling-Card Stories

Here are what others shared with me about their calling cards, to give you an idea of the varied ways the universe can reach out to us all. These stories illustrate how spirits and energies from the nonphysical realm can communicate with us through subtle and meaningful signs. Whether it's through a TV show, animals, numbers, or symbols, these experiences remind us of the loving presence and guidance that surrounds us. Embracing these signs allows us to feel more connected to the unseen world and reinforces the belief that we are supported and guided on our life's journey.

Natalie

After my friend Jesse passed away, I began noticing signs related to his love for the show *Golden Girls*. On New Year's Eve in Nashville, while visiting my boyfriend's cousins, we were greeted by a life-sized Golden Girls cut-out in their window. It felt like a clear sign from Jesse.

Shannon

For me, hummingbirds are a symbol of my grandmother's presence in my life. She loved hummingbirds and would always have special feeders in her yard for them. She would sit with me and watch them fly up for hours. I cherish those memories, and when I'm having a hard day and I see one at my window, I know that she is there, reassuring me.

Meredith

Whenever I see white cars with horse logos, it feels like a connection to my divine masculine. My grandpa also had a deep connection to both horses and cars, so I see him in both.

Brett

My grandfather was born on April 13. He would always get so upset when people would say the number thirteen would bring bad fortune. He always said it was his lucky number, and he told me to always believe it would bring me luck, too. When I discovered Taylor Swift and found out that that was also her number, I was like "whoa."

My grandfather was also a huge New York Mets fan. On the day of his funeral, the Mets won 13–1, which is a rare score for baseball. But we felt like it was definitely a sign because of his connection to the team— we even had flowers shaped like the Mets logo at his funeral. So seeing it made me feel like he was still around, and it still does whenever it shows up today.

stay present and aware of the love and support available to us when we embrace the unseen energies and possibilities around us.

The next few sections cover common symbols and ways to decipher them when they surface in your daily life.

Animal Calling Cards

There are many different ways for animal calling cards to show up in your life. They don't have to be literal, physical animals that you might see on a walk in the woods, although that would be a powerful occurrence. However, it's more likely in our modern world for you to see these animals represented as motifs—on clothing, on TV, in the lyrics of songs, or in dreams. Here are some animals that can carry strong spiritual messages, so that the next time you see them—in whatever way they come to you—you'll know how to interpret their presence.

BATS: Because bats are nocturnal animals, they're often said to represent the literal darkness of night, as well as the potential that you are hiding from something. The bat can be a signal that it's time to face your fears. Bats are the only flying mammals, and all flight implies the symbolism of rising above. In that way, they are a symbol of hope, and their appearance ensures you that you will be able to fly, even after you go through changes that may be awkward and abrupt. Bats are social and live in flocks; so if you see a bat, the universe might be telling you to spend more time with friends and family. The saying "blind as a bat" is misleading, because bats aren't blind at all! In reality, they are experts at navigating through darkness and can remind you to use your own personal sonar to feel your way through situations that may be confusing, like they use their sensitive noses to guide them like a GPS. If bats are appearing to you, it could be a signal to focus on your clairaudient "clear-hearing" abilities. The bat signifies intuition, so take it as a signal to tap in to your extrasensory abilities in order to uncover the truth, especially if you feel that there might be something in your life that has not yet been uncovered.

BEARS: If you feel exhausted and depleted, bears can teach you how to draw from previously untapped energy reserves to replenish yourself. When the bear sleeps during the winter, its kidneys shut down completely. Metaphysically, the kidneys represent discernment, so the bear can be a powerful signal to make a decision and trust what may happen next. Female bears actually give birth while they are sleeping, leaving the newborn cubs to fend for themselves immediately. When a bear appears as a calling card, the universe is asking you to be aware of your judgment and ability to evaluate what is around you currently so that you and your ideas (like the sleeping bear's cubs) are safe. A bear tells you to emerge from the comfortable cave in which you've been hibernating and give birth to those new ideas you have been nurturing for some time. They are ready to live on their own!

BISON: What we know as the buffalo or the American buffalo is a bison. These massive beings can weigh up to a ton and a half and have prominent humped shoulders. The bison teaches us that abundance is available if we know how to access it. The bison is also unpredictable and dangerous, and can symbolize the need to stay grounded when you start to experience more prosperity. Due to its size, the bison is said to typically follow the most straightforward path through a landscape, so its presence may suggest that it is not the time for you to move in head-first. Rather, some form of prosperity may be coming to you on an easy path, so all you have to do is wait.

CATS: The cat has been written about in a million different ways, and a number of qualities have been ascribed to it; so if you see a cat or feel its presence strongly in your life, it's best to think closely about which quality is emerging most for you. In ancient Egypt, the goddess Bast is portrayed as a woman with a cat's head, and was revered. However, cats can be associated with fear, as they have inspired it in humans—they emerge mysteriously from the dark of night, or their yowls are heard at midnight and can seem sinister. Cats have been shunned and depicted as evil throughout history. If you feel fear or anxiety when seeing cats, investigate whether you are avoiding something stressful or scary. More traditionally, cats can represent mystery and magic. They remind us to be aware of what we cannot see. Paying attention to what a cat is doing could give you clues as to what they are trying to tell you. It could also be a call to look closer in order to more effectively evaluate your life: a cat's retinas have more rods, which enhances their ability to perceive light and allows them to effectively see in the dark. When a cat appears in your life, magical things may happen.

COYOTES: The coyote can make a den anywhere; so if you see one, it may be a sign that you have a roaming spirit about you. Maybe it means that you're the "home is wherever you make it" type. Still, coyotes have a family unit that represents closeness and loyalty. They mate for life, and the father is the one who cares for the young. And while every coyote is a hunter, they understand the value of a team. Coyotes hunt in relays, with one beginning and then handing off the task to the next in the pack, so that they are able to more efficiently track down prey. All this is to say that a coyote can paradoxically be a sign of both independence and cooperation, whether in a family, friendship, workplace, or intimate partnership. Remember who you are, but also acknowledge how much more can be done when you work with others. Finally, the coyote can also be a sign of despair—when you hear its famous howl, it can be a warning of danger, a call for help, or an expression of loneliness.

DEER: Because it is a prey animal, the deer has very acute senses that help it understand whether it's in a safe or unsafe environment. The deer symbolizes the need for you to be even more aware of your surroundings than you already are—something may be threatening you that you're not yet aware of. What is not being said directly to you at this time? Read between the lines and trust your gut. The deer stays with its young for the first few days of life, barely moving. This is a reminder for you to be gentle with yourself and with others around you.

DOGS: The dog represents loyalty because of the strong bonds it forms with its owners, as well as with other dogs. Descendants of coyotes and wolves, dogs are pack animals who understand the concept of service to others. However, because there are so many types of dogs, it is important to dive deeper into the different types of dog characteristics you encounter. What breed is surfacing for you? A service dog like a German shepherd? A small dog like a poodle, which has a stronger association with fun and companionship? Does the dog seem threatening, or is it standing by you and protecting you? The dog can be one of the purest symbols of unconditional love—it could mean that some presence is standing with you and keeping you from harm—but dogs can also be ruthless guardians who will attack anyone who threatens their territory. If you see a dog with that aura, it could mean that you need to stand your ground against those who would hurt you.

DOLPHINS: Swimming so gracefully through the water, dolphins symbolize the ability to become rhythmic in life. If you see a dolphin, you may want to ask yourself how you can navigate challenges as effortlessly. You may be inspired to start a breathwork or meditation practice. The dolphin is an intelligent creature and one of the only creatures other than humans which seeks out pleasure. Seeing dolphins may mean it is time to look at the sources of tension in your existence and seek out the things that will breathe new life into you.

HUMMINGBIRDS: Hummingbirds remind us to sing and be joyful. It is also a sign of longevity, and of the passage of time. The hummingbird can move its wings in a figure-eight pattern, which symbolizes infinity but also the continuous motion of past and future. Seeing a hummingbird can also mean that there are sources of joy in your life that you have been overlooking. Because the hummingbird uses its long tongue to draw the nectar out of the depths of flowers, its presence can mean that you have a sweetness that hasn't been tapped into yet. The hummingbird also has the ability to fly sideways, backward, and forward. There are not any other birds that can fly backward, so the hummingbird is quite special in the way that it can control its flight. In the same way, the universe may be asking you to move intentionally and make informed choices about your next steps. Hummingbirds like to be free and alone, except when it is time for a mate—so if you're considering a new relationship, be absolutely sure about committing. Each hummingbird nest is a masterpiece of architectural ability, so the hummingbird can also be a reminder to take pride in the home you have built for yourself. This bird is a symbol that nothing is impossible. You can do whatever you want as long as you put your mind to it!

Numerical Calling Cards

When you see numbers that you believe are calling cards from the universe, intentionally ask for more signs. Ask for clarity, or ask for more information. Explore the vibration of each of the numbers from zero to ten in the section beginning on page 80. When you see repeating sequences of these numbers, remember the defining qualities that each holds and what place it is in where you observe it. Pythagoras stated that each number has its own meaning and vibration and that everything is mathematically precise.

It's not a coincidence when you see 11:11 or 444—it's a download, and you are ready to update your software.

First, to understand numerical calling cards, you must have a basic understanding of numerology.

Numerology is the study of the mystical connection between numbers and the cosmos.

The roots of numerology can be traced back to Pythagorean theory and philosophy. Pythagoras, the ancient Greek mathematician, philosopher, and spiritual teacher, believed that numbers held a profound significance and were the essence of all creation. According to Pythagorean teachings, each number possessed unique qualities and vibrations that influenced both the material and spiritual realms. This belief laid the foundation for numerology, where numbers are seen as symbols of divine energy and carry specific meanings and influences. By studying the patterns and symbolism of numbers, practitioners of numerology seek to gain insights into the deeper aspects of life, spirituality, and the universe. Thus, Pythagorean philosophy provided the philosophical framework from which numerology emerged, making it an enduring and influential practice for understanding the mysteries of existence. The most basic principle of numerology is that everything vibrates at a certain frequency, and, within each of those frequencies, you can find hidden energies that can guide you in working with your life.

So convinced was Pythagoras of the significance of the power of numbers that he founded the Pythagorean Academy, where he taught and guided students in decoding what he considered to be the language of the universe. In the metaphysical mindset, numerology serves as a powerful tool to uncover deeper insights into our lives and connect with the subtle energies that shape our reality. He taught that everything in time and space could be expressed through numbers similar to code. But what most people don't know is that after Pythagoras's death, his theories were not taught or even spoken about for centuries. Pythagoras had claimed that he was the incarnated son of the Greek god Hermes, and that it was in his past life that he could have been given these powers.

In numerology, as in Pythagorean philosophy, each number has a specific energetic makeup:

ZERO: The spiritual meaning of the number zero is one of unlimited potential. Zero is the void where ideas circulate and nothing is truly formed yet. The form of the number zero is of the womb, representing the openness that comes with endless energy and realities. The number zero also represents the spiritual meaning of things always being in flow. Zero is a receptive energy.

ONE: The number one is a strong symbol of individuality and the beginning of a new self-discovery. When you encounter the number one, you are becoming more empowered as the self. One is the essence of your individuality. It is also the constant search to find and define yourself. The one represents the potential to learn to know the self, ultimately aligning you to be objective and see life from the perspective of your higher self.

TWO: The spiritual meaning of the number two is that of union of yin and yang energy. It is the number of balance, and a reminder that there is a cocreation and cooperating aspect to everything. When the number two shows up for you, you are being told that you will soon know of some new form. This could mean change in your life is coming: maybe this is in your financial realm or in the realm of family. The meaning of the number two says that to create something, you must generate a cocreative environment. The number one cannot create by itself; it must be with another of itself to create the two. This is amplified when you see the number two along with the two number ones.

THREE: The number three is the triangle, which is the foundation of every aspect in the known world. As a geometric shape, it plays a fundamental and essential role in various aspects of our physical reality. In mathematics and geometry, the triangle is one of the most basic shapes, consisting of three sides and three angles. This simplicity and versatility make triangles the building blocks for more complex shapes and structures.

In the natural world, triangles can be found in various forms, such as in the structure of crystals, the arrangement of atoms in molecules, the patterns of flower petals, and the shapes of leaves and trees. Triangles also appear in architecture, where they provide stability and balance in construction, and in various art forms as a fundamental element of design.

Three is the number of movement. Three shows that there are energies flowing. Magic begins to reveal itself as a spinning vortex when the number three is introduced. The number three has many divine aspects: the Father, the Son, and the Holy Ghost; the mind, body, and spirit. The energies of the number three set things in motion for you. With the numbers one and two, you started to cocreate. The number three sets those things into motion. Positive thoughts and intentional activations will continue to draw these positive energies and opportunities back to you. When you see the number three along with the numbers two and one, or you see any combination of numbers that adds up to three, remember that this is your sign that magic is happening all around you because you are the cocreator. You have put out this electromagnetic signature and it will come back to you.

FOUR: The spiritual meaning of the number four is one of foundation. It is the physical structure and the organization in the physical world that the mind, body, and spirit need. We see this in many aspects of nature and culture, such as the medicine wheel and the four seasons and the four chambers of the heart. Four symbolizes the home and the need for stability. The vibrational nature of the number four creates the ability for a sacred space inside your home or the home of another. Whether you are traveling or are at home, you must find a place to connect to yourself and to your own foundation. This could be a place to meditate or a place to take a leisurely walk. Strengthening and finding the foundation of the self is a very prominent part of the number four, and something to consider when it comes up.

FIVE: The number five is the number of abundance and the number of manifestations in action. It is the five elements: earth, air, fire, water, and ether. With the five, you can manifest with all the components that you have at your disposal. The vibrational meaning of five aligns with the freedom to fulfill your heart's desire and follow your bliss. The five is representing pure faith and having a connection to the synergistic forces of nature and the universe.

SIX: The number six has gotten a bad reputation, but it is the number of seeing. A negative connotation exists in some cultures and belief systems, due to various historical and cultural associations. One of the main reasons for this negative reputation is its connection to the concept of "the number of the beast" mentioned in the Bible's book of Revelation. In Christian tradition, the number 666 is associated with evil and the Devil. The passage in Revelation 13:18 states: "This calls for wisdom: let the one who has understanding calculate the number of the beast, for it is the number of a man, and his number is 666." As a result, the number 6, especially when repeated three times (666), became widely associated with malevolence and darkness. The number itself connects you to your inner guidance. If you are seeing the number six, this is because the realm of intuition is trying to break through for you so that you can activate your clairvoyance. Six is the number that tells you anything is possible—it is aligned with imagination and dreams. This number is a gateway to unlocking and embracing the intuitive abilities that each of us possesses. Creating a vision and holding it in your mind when you see the number six can help you bring your desires from the ethereal into the physical realm.

SEVEN: The number seven holds an extremely special and divine vibration. Seven has been attributed to the enlightened powers of the rainbow, of the chakras, and of all the clairs (the extrasensory abilities we all possess to see, hear, feel, taste, and know beyond our physical experience). Seven is serendipity. When you see the number seven, you can feel good about luck being on your side: you are an electromagnetic frequency aligning to luck. Seven is a reminder to trust your intuitive feelings and practice them. Be willing to be guided. Inviting more synchronicities to show up for you when you see the number seven is always a great way to get even more clarity.

EIGHT: The vibrational impact of the number eight is one of infinite possibilities and abundance. It is infinite prosperity, which is everywhere in the universe. The vibrational meaning of the number eight is realized through self-empowerment. With the right action, you can create what you conceive. Eight is the number that supplies the prosperous flow of money, but also positive actions, fortuitous meetings, inspired alignments, and situations that lead to good things.

NINE: The number nine is one of cosmic consciousness. Nikola Tesla stated that if you could understand meanings of the numbers three, six, and nine, you would unlock the secrets to the universe. The number nine is considered a very special doorway to awakening the highest self and to aligning with what truly is for the highest good. The number nine opens you up to the unlimited potential that is your highest self. When you see the number nine, it is your divine purpose being revealed to you. It asks you to change what is happening in order to walk through a doorway to your higher self. You have always realized that you are a unique individual, and you have your own purpose when you see the number nine: it is reminding you of this higher calling, and it is telling you it is time to teach.

TEN: This one is a bonus. The number ten is the number of completion, and it is the number of the destiny within the universe. The universal language is called binary code, and this binary code is information that is comprised of only ones and zeros in an unlimited number of combinations. Therefore, the actual vibrational essence of the number ten shows that what is written in the binary code is also written in the stars. It is your heartbeat, it is your messages, it is everything that is you, your talents, your intuition . . . all coming together to create one expression of cocreation. The number ten is an invitation to cocreate with the universe and a sign that you are being guided by a universal code that awakens you to the unlimited possibilities that are available for you as an energetic being.

PART 2
Mindset Rituals

"How you think and how you feel literally creates your personal reality."

—Dr. Joe Dispenza, *Becoming Supernatural*

You've learned how the universe works and have begun to start reaching out to it—past space and time, into the quantum field. You've started to chart how the universe reaches back in the form of ethereal calling cards. So this is where we get into the really juicy part of the book. Your mind is ready to build more, to start perceiving new realities. These physical rituals will help you take the inspired action you need throughout your day. Reminder: take your time, and don't be so hard on yourself. You're ready.

Every single day, you don't wake up and think "I only get to take 186,000 breaths in my life. I'd better make sure that I use every single breath and don't let any of them go to waste." You wake up and you realize that you can breathe as much as you want, and you live as if you have an unlimited amount of breaths to take. So why do we worry that nothing else in our life is as unlimited as our ability to breathe? Instead of feeling this abundance, we wake up and immediately start thinking of all the stressful things that we must do, and every part of our mindset becomes fixated on these tasks, creating a physical stress response. Instead of getting out of bed and beginning to experience the day, so many of us immediately pull out our phones and get on Instagram, training our brains to agonize over what everyone else is doing. So, this is my invitation for you to stop and make a change. The following pages are a place for you to begin to establish some new mindset rituals. Holding and creating a space for yourself can take as little as five minutes.

I'm going to expand on jewelry, household chores, and even the deeper concepts like reading tarot cards and learning about your past life, including the Akashic records. These can be new ways for you to recalibrate your mind and remind yourself that you are an infinite, powerful, cocreative being.

CHAPTER 6

GLAMORIZE YOUR LIFE

When you look good, you feel good; and when you feel good, you attract good. Before I ever realized that this was an actual form of neurological reprogramming, I was dressing myself up to feel better. When you grow up in a neighborhood where everyone has a huge lack of consciousness and an extreme life view that doesn't stay up to your standards, your mind has to do something. So I would cut up my clothes and make new designs, and then I would take photos of them and create little fashion shows for myself. This burst of creative energy that would happen any time I was feeling sad or lonely would help me glamorize myself, which I began to realize was having a major effect not just on my mood, but on all the things around me.

When I was trying on new accessories or clothing, I may have noticed that I looked amazing, but what I didn't realize was that this actively changed my electromagnetic field. I remember my grandmother—we called her mammaw (to pronounce it, it sounds like a goat bleating and the sound "aww") "maaaa mawww." I don't recall ever seeing this woman without a full face of makeup and her hair completely done up from the time I was three years old until the day she passed away before my seventeenth birthday. She must have embedded the energetic power of adornment into me without my even knowing.

When the COVID-19 pandemic hit and everything changed for everyone as we knew it, I made it a daily practice to adorn myself with jewelry that made me feel empowered and less lonely. Every day, even if I didn't put makeup on, I made it a point to wear jewelry. I wanted to elicit a certain emotional experience; therefore, I used what I had at my disposal to create that experience for my brain. One gift that my partner always gives me is jewelry. The pieces that he picks are gorgeous and layered; and, during the long-distance phase of our relationship, I would wear them every day to feel closer to him. Two months into the pandemic, we moved into our home in California together, and I still never leave the house without wearing a piece of jewelry from him. Was I subconsciously creating the space for this manifestation to come to fruition? Maybe. I was very aware of how I felt when I was sitting around in sweatpants with no jewelry versus when I was fully put together. You might be super-productive in your sweatpants and your Nikes, and that's your glamour! It's finding what works for you.

The Glamour of Being Authentically Yourself

One of my best friends, Alex, is an ultimate glamorizer of life, and she is never not in sneakers—but you better believe they are the cutest! For Alex, glamour means being authentically herself. So a glamorous night might begin with a fantastic dinner and end with a good book, a little OG in her bong, and her cozy bed. Sometimes it just gets "too people-y" for her, and this is where she goes for comfort. This glamour consists of her hair up in a messy bun, an oversized T-shirt, and some comfortable leggings.

Ask yourself, how can you be the most authentic version of who you are, so that your metaphysical self shines through in your clothing, accessories, hair, and movement? Does that mean big hair, red lips, and high heels (or a slick suit, bespoke shoes, and cologne), or does it mean a fluffy blanket and your favorite movie? Be intentional, and you will find that great things will happen.

The Glamour of a Good Manifestation

This advice may sound somewhat familiar, because its principles correspond with so many of the laws of the universe, not least of which is the Law of Attraction. So whether you're getting all dolled up or are just the comfiest version of yourself, you'll find that it will put you in the perfect place to manifest.

Take, for example, my aforementioned friend Alex. One evening as she was getting ready to get all her-version-of-glammed for bed, she decided she was going to write in her journal as her "new self." The "new self" would be the person who had solved her problems and was successful in her goals. The big goal she wrote down was this: "GET OUT OF DEBT THIS YEAR!"

This seemed daunting, but she was determined to really achieve her dream. Now, before I tell you what happened, I want you to know that these results may not be typical, but this is a real experience that had all the right puzzle pieces in order for something extraordinary to happen. Alex wrote down in her journal that night what she would do *when* she achieved this goal, how she would feel, and what her life would be like *in the future*. And when she went to sleep, she let it all go and believed that this potential was already on its way to her. She woke up the next morning to see that someone she had known for a decade who owed her a not-insignificant amount of money (less than $100K but more than $30K) had finally, unexpectedly, paid her back. She was immediately able to pay off all of her debt—her journaling had led her to a place where she was living as that person she envisioned. And this took less than twelve hours.

How did she do it? The first step was physically becoming this "new self": more confident, more comfortable, and less apologetic. She created a physical space for her dreams to manifest. And then by journaling, she gave herself space to emotionally assume the role of that person. So it wasn't entirely out of the ordinary that this person repaid her. And if you've ever lent money to a friend, you know how uncommon it can be to get it back!

How Can I Adorn Myself?

There are many ways that you can take the first step of physically becoming who you want to be. It's definitely not limited to jewelry, but it can be anything that feels right for you: tattoos, piercings, scarves, makeup, going to the gym, hair extensions. Maybe your idea of glamour is a seventeen-step smoothie and a fifteen-step skin-care routine. Whatever it is . . . get it.

The idea at the root of this practice is to create a vibrational change in your physical being and your immediate environment. Glamour energy can create massive shifts in your mindset, and subsequently your reality. To learn more on glamour magic, refer to the References and Resources sections in the back of the book—there are some great resources there, including my favorite, *Glamour Witch,* by Sophie Saint Thomas.

Glamour magic can consist of the following:

- The clothes you wear
- Your hair style and color
- The jewelry you choose or choose not to wear
- The way you like your nails
- Your skincare routine
- Your bathing routine
- Your makeup routine
- The body modifications of your choice (piercings, tattoos, etc.)

The sky's pretty much the limit—don't relegate yourself to just "nice clothes, nice jewelry," although that's a great place to start.

RADIANT GLAMOUR RITUAL: EMBRACING YOUR INNER LIGHT

This short glamour ritual is designed to empower you with confidence and self-love as you embrace your inner radiance. By dressing up in colors that resonate with your intentions and speaking affirmations in the mirror, you will create a powerful energy shift that enhances your self-expression and positive mindset.

Materials Needed:
A selection of clothes and accessories in your chosen colors
A full-length mirror

Setting the Space:
Choose a peaceful and private space where you can perform this ritual without distractions. Dim the lights or light a few candles to create a serene ambiance.

Selecting the Colors:
Choose clothes and accessories in colors that align with your intentions for the day. For example, red for passion and confidence, blue for calm and communication, green for growth and healing, or yellow for creativity and joy. Trust your intuition to guide you in selecting the perfect hues for your mood and goals.

Dressing with Intention:
Begin to dress yourself in the chosen colors mindfully. As you put on each garment and accessory, imagine that you are adorning yourself with the energy of these colors, and feel their empowering qualities infusing your being.

Affirmations in the Mirror:

Stand in front of the mirror and take a deep breath to center yourself. Look into your own eyes and speak empowering affirmations out loud. Customize these affirmations to resonate with your unique intentions for the day. For example:

"I am confident and capable. I radiate self-assurance and grace."

"I embrace my creativity and let it flow effortlessly in all I do."

"I am worthy of love and acceptance. I am deserving of all the good that comes my way."

"I am a beacon of positivity and joy. My presence brightens the lives of others."

Embodying Your Radiance:

With each affirmation, let your posture reflect the power of your words. Stand tall, shoulders back, and visualize a radiant light emanating from within you. Put your hands on your hips and stand in that "power stance." Embrace the energy of the colors you are wearing, and allow their qualities to amplify your intentions.

Appreciation and Gratitude:

Take a moment to appreciate your unique beauty and the powerful intentions you have set. Express gratitude for your inner strength and the opportunity to embrace your authentic self.

Carry Your Radiance:

Carry the energy of this glamour ritual with you throughout the day. Walk around as this "new self." Whenever you need a boost of confidence or positivity, return to the affirmations and the colors you adorned yourself with, knowing that you hold the power to embody your inner light. Whenever you walk by a mirror, make eye contact with yourself and remind yourself of the affirmations.

Through this short and powerful glamour ritual, you have activated an inner radiance and set the stage for a day filled with self-expression and empowerment. Remember, the colors you wear and the affirmations you speak are tools that can uplift your emotional state and inspire a positive mindset. Embrace your authentic self and don't be afraid to try something new.

Color Magic

Glamour doesn't have to be something you are putting on your body, but can also be the colors surrounding your body. Colors have a psychological effect on our minds. This is why certain colors are used in advertising: red for passion, yellow for energy, and so on. It doesn't matter if it's an ad for a hamburger, a car, or a new kind of lipstick: colors motivate us to buy what they're selling and assume the fantasy that those items promise.

Having a distinct eye for what colors to paint your walls or wear is a talent in its own right. Study the traditional associations between colors and certain properties (again, refer to the References and Resources sections for some great resources) and you will gain some fascinating insight into the emotional and spiritual properties of colors, as well as correspondences that have been created through tradition. For example, using color as a means of restricting certain levels of status has been in effect for many years, including in the time of Queen Elizabeth I, where wearing purple outside of the court of her royal subjects was punishable. This rule created the association between purple and royalty, which still holds true today in the ceremonial clothes of kings and queens.

You could also try wearing colors you might not normally feel drawn to in order to glamorize your life. For example, if you're usually an earth-tone person, try breaking out of your routine and wearing red. Red is the color that we associate with lust and confidence. Science talks about the "red-dress effect"—or in *The Matrix,* where Morpheus says "Always be aware of the woman in the red dress," which suggests that wearing red is recognized by humans more than other colors.

GLAMOUR MEDITATION

In this guided meditation, we will explore the art of using clothes, jewelry, and makeup as tools for glamorizing our lives and embracing a metaphysical mindset. Through the act of adorning ourselves with intention and creativity, we can tap into our inner power, elevate our confidence, and express our authentic selves. Let this visualization guide you on a transformative journey of self-expression and empowerment.

Find a quiet and comfortable space where you can fully immerse yourself in this meditation. Sit or lie down in a relaxed position, and take a few deep breaths to center yourself.

Imagine yourself standing in front of a large mirror, a reflection of your true self waiting to be revealed. Surrounding you is an array of clothes, jewelry, and makeup items, each representing a unique facet of your personality and desires.

Take a moment to set your intention for this meditation. Decide what aspect of yourself you want to emphasize, or what emotion you want to invoke, through your chosen adornments. Is it confidence, grace, creativity, or love? Trust your instincts in selecting the pieces that resonate with your intention.

As you begin to select and wear your chosen items, feel the transformative energy they exude. Each garment, each piece of jewelry, and every brush of makeup enhances the radiance of your being, inviting you to embrace your inner light.

Imagine your reflection taking on the essence of powerful archetypes that inspire you—goddesses, queens, and legendary figures from mythology and history. Feel their wisdom, strength, and beauty flowing through you as you integrate their qualities into your being.

Visualize friends or colleagues sharing their stories of how glamorizing their lives helped them embrace a metaphysical mindset. Hear tales of how a friend felt more connected to her creativity through a carefully chosen pendant, or how a colleague found a renewed sense of purpose by dressing with intention for important meetings.

With every garment, piece of jewelry, or stroke of makeup, feel your confidence growing. Acknowledge that true beauty comes from within and that adorning yourself is an external reflection of your internal radiance.

As you explore different adornments, recognize that this is an opportunity to express your authentic self and unique style. Embrace the joy of self-discovery and the freedom to express who you are without limitation.

Take a moment to express gratitude for the abundance of choices and the opportunity to use clothes, jewelry, and makeup as tools for self-expression and empowerment.

With a renewed sense of self-awareness and empowerment, thank yourself for taking this transformative journey. Slowly bring your awareness back to the present moment, knowing that you can tap into this metaphysical mindset whenever you choose to do so.

As you step away from the mirror, remember that glamorizing your life is not merely about appearance, but is also about embracing the depths of your being. Your clothes, jewelry, and makeup become symbols of self-expression and empowerment, guiding you on a path of metaphysical transformation. Embrace the power of adorning yourself with intention, and let your inner light shine brightly, illuminating your path with grace and beauty.

CHAPTER 7

ALCHEMIZE DAILY

lchemy is associated with experiments meant to turn common products into precious metals like gold. Sometimes known as the medieval precursor to modern chemistry, its underlying belief was that it was possible to change one substance into another. In this chapter, I won't be describing how to create the elixir of life or turn iron into a precious metal. Rather, I'm suggesting that it's possible to change your perception of your life through repeated inspired actions. Spiritual alchemy is a philosophy whose end goal is self-transformation. By shifting your perception, it's possible to reevaluate your life, creating an immense amount of gratitude, and therefore a shift in your electromagnetic field that adds a bit of spiritual enlightenment to what might have seemed insignificant or even unpleasant.

One of the best tools for shifting your perspective when faced with a daily task you simply don't want to do is to ask the questions: "What is this teaching me? What can I take away from how I am feeling in this moment?" What was once a task you would rather avoid becomes something that brings more familiarity with who you really are. Reframing situations with these questions can give you information about where this feeling originated from. Maybe you were forced to clean on certain days when you were a child, or maybe you were forced to read during summer break; so whenever doing these tasks as an adult comes up, you feel as if it's an obligation and your mind starts to persuade you to back away from the uncomfortable. But what if you started the entire day out differently?

Instead of waking up and grabbing your phone to check your missed texts and emails, you open your eyes and say "How can today be the best day? How will I see the world today: as an unlimited opportunity, or as a burden?" Every minute after you wake up, you have choices to make: Do you stay in the bed, do you hit the snooze, do you reach for your phone, do you jump up and get right in the shower, do you roll over and kiss your partner? These choices set the tone for the entire day and sometimes the remainder of your life if you are a creature of habit. Imagine how much fulfillment you could bring into your life by making small intentional acts to alchemize your perspective! Instead of dreading the emails, express gratitude that so many people want your expertise. Instead of grabbing your phone immediately, grab your pen, and journal your first thoughts or any dreams you remember upon waking. Rather than sneak away so you don't wake your partner, snuggle up next to them so they wake up feeling your loving intention. Alchemizing daily is about understanding the discourse you experience in your day-to-day life. By becoming aware of the tasks that bring strong feelings during your day, you can establish a new set of patterns that benefit you instead of ones that leave you feeling drained at the end of the day. You start living in a state that is your creating a new foundation that ripples out to everyone.

So, what does this mean in terms of your day-to-day life? Cleaning the baseboards?! Yes, it's possible to add enlightenment to your life just by doing daily chores. In other words, my mom would have loved this chapter! But it's true: those little tasks that you may do without thinking are an opportunity to create a regular practice that can change your mindset. When we were younger, chores were framed as something we had to do, or else. But what would happen if we looked at them as something we might *want* to do instead of something we're *obligated* to do?

If you're like me, there are some chores you just can't stand, or do reluctantly because they're necessary. For example, in my new house, we have a dishwasher. However, I did not grow up with a dishwasher. That's not something that we had in government housing in Tennessee, so it doesn't interest me. Handwashing, however, is something that I did grow up with. That's the chore I choose to do in order to alchemize daily.

When I was a kid, we washed the dishes by hand, filling the sink up with water. This is how my grandmother taught me; and if you were in the kitchen, she let you know that you'd better be putting yourself to use. From a young age, I realized that I really enjoyed washing and cleansing and drying and putting away the dishes: I enjoyed the ritual and was glad to be useful to my grandmother. So for me, one way I alchemize energy daily is to hand-wash the dishes, even though it would probably be faster to just throw them in the dishwasher.

Likewise, folding the laundry is a meditative process for me. Pretty sure J. Cole said it the best: "I want to fold clothes for you." The methodical process of removing warm, clean clothes from the dryer and arranging them into neat stacks makes me feel accomplished and useful. Reframing the importance of domestic tasks is crucial, as it empowers us to see these tasks as meaningful and valuable contributions to our well-being and our home environment. By understanding the significance of these daily chores, we can approach them with a positive mindset, viewing them as opportunities for self-care, creating a comfortable living space, and fostering a sense of fulfillment in nurturing our home and family. Embracing this perspective allows us to find joy and satisfaction in our daily routines, making these tasks an integral part of our overall well-being and happiness.

Everyday Meditation

Whenever something that is a normal process for you becomes meditative, you unlock a part of yourself in which you can create space for new things to come in. You're firing a new neural pathway because you're not seeing your daily activities as a burden or an obligation. Author Dr. Joe Dispenza specifically talks about how meditation means "to become familiar with." If you are performing an activity that enables you to become more familiar with yourself, that can become meditation.

Does that mean that all simple tasks are meditations? Sit back for a moment and think about the things that you do during the day. Many may put you into a meditative or trancelike state. Write down the things that do this for you. That could be making your coffee or tea in the morning, cooking breakfast for your children or packing their lunch, applying makeup, writing your to-do list for the day, wiping down the counters . . .

the list can go on and on. Go through each room of your house and list activities that put you into a trancelike state. For example:

Bathroom: your makeup, skin-care routine, shower routine.

Kitchen: washing the dishes and putting them away, chopping vegetables, stirring soup.

Bedroom: making the bed, reading before going to sleep, stretching when you wake up.

You can alchemize your daily life by being aware in the present moment that what you're doing is creating a meditative state. So when you go on autopilot and push yourself through a task, you are not alchemizing—you are running on the automatic program. However, when you take the time to truly be present as you complete the task and hold an intention, you are giving yourself that opportunity to experience the process that transforms your mindset. Alchemy is the ancient practice that combines elements of science, philosophy, and mysticism, with the goal of transforming and perfecting both physical substances and the self.

So, with the knowledge you learned in the first chapter about how your mind is matter in motion, alchemizing your life means you're changing one part of your life into something different. This could be a simple switch in the perspective, which is why I'm asking you to reevaluate everyday activities to create small, constant changes—tiny alchemical transformations that can lead up to the kinds of major manifestations you may be hoping to create. I am suggesting that you engage in this practice to help them discover the power of transforming their everyday experiences into opportunities for personal growth and self-improvement. By reframing your mindset and approach to daily tasks, readers can cultivate a sense of mindfulness and intentionality in your actions. As you consistently apply this perspective in your lives, you will notice a positive shift in their overall well-being, finding greater contentment and fulfillment in the seemingly mundane aspects of your daily routines. Over time, this regular practice of reframing and infusing intention into daily tasks can lead to a deeper connection with oneself and a heightened appreciation for the little joys that life has to offer. It is a journey of self-discovery and empowerment, ultimately leading to a more fulfilling and enriched life experience.

SWEEPING THE PATH OF CLARITY: A MEDITATION OF RENEWAL

In this meditation, we will explore the transformative power of sweeping, using this simple household chore to create inner clarity and renewal. Just as we sweep away dust and debris from our physical space, we can also release mental and emotional clutter, paving the way for a fresh perspective on life. Embrace the mindful rhythm of sweeping as you cultivate a sense of peace, harmony, and revitalization within.

1. **Preparation:** Find a quiet space where you can focus on the act of sweeping without distractions. Stand tall, with your feet rooted to the ground, and take a few deep breaths to center yourself in the present moment.

2. **Embrace the Broom:** Hold the broom with both hands, feeling its texture, weight, and energy. Connect with it as a tool of transformation, a vessel for sweeping away the old and making space for the new.

3. **Grounding:** As you begin to sweep, visualize roots extending from the soles of your feet, reaching deep into the Earth. With each stroke, draw in the grounding energy of the Earth, anchoring yourself firmly in the present.

4. **Sweep with Intention:** With each sweep of the broom, set an intention to release mental and emotional clutter. Imagine the broom gathering up not just physical dust but also thoughts, worries, and tensions that no longer serve you.

5. **Mindful Movements:** Allow your body to move in harmony with the sweeping motion. Feel the flow of energy as you sweep, and let the rhythm become a dance of mindfulness and grace.

6. Letting Go: As you collect the dirt and debris, visualize the broom absorbing everything that you wish to release. With each sweep, let go of negative thoughts, doubts, and emotional baggage.

7. Focus on the Breath: Breathe deeply and slowly as you sweep, using your breath to anchor you in the present moment. Inhale clarity and renewal, and exhale any residual tension or negativity.

8. Cleansing Visualization: Envision your living space being filled with a bright, cleansing light. As you sweep, see this light dispelling darkness and stagnation, leaving behind a renewed and vibrant atmosphere.

9. Gratitude for Renewal: As you finish sweeping, take a moment to express gratitude for the newfound clarity and freshness in your space and within yourself. Acknowledge the power of intention and mindfulness.

10. Embrace the New: Step back and observe the clean and clear path before you. See it as a reflection of your inner state—renewed, focused, and ready for the next phase of your journey.

As you go about your daily chores, remember that every task can be an opportunity for self-discovery and inner peace. Embrace the mindfulness of sweeping and let it be a reminder of your power to create positive change in both your external and internal worlds. You are now walking the path of clarity and renewal with purpose and grace.

CHAPTER 8

VACATION AT THE VOID

I n Dr. Joe Dispenza's book *Becoming Supernatural,* he addresses that by the time you are 35 years old, you have developed a programmed personality based on your past experiences. Because of the "thinking–feeling–acting" loop that you continually create based on your past, you develop a series of automatic emotional reactions, thoughts, and attitudes. He states that 95 percent of who we are by a certain age is a habituated set of programs in which we have trained the body to be programmed by the mind. Instead of the conscious mind "running the show," the body is doing so. This means that only 5 percent of who you are is "conscious," while the other 95 percent is being run by the subconscious. What if we could tap into the subconscious to help create our future? What if there were ways to unlock portions of that 95 percent?

Let's take a look at the past in this chapter, all about past-life regression and the Akashic records.

Past-life regression is rooted in the concept of reincarnation, which has been embraced by religions and belief systems throughout history. The belief that your one immutable soul is brought back into consciousness over and over again throughout many lifetimes is one that has found its way into many different timelines and across cultures, from Hinduism—where the soul's many rebirths are dictated by karma—to the philosophers of ancient Greece. In the twentieth century, the renowned psychic medium Edgar Cayce wrote extensively about reincarnation, believing that, much as in Hindu beliefs, the soul was given multiple new lives. His belief was that each renewed existence was motivated by a soul's desire to learn new lessons.

Cayce also developed the concept of the Akashic records, which are often referred to as the "Book of Life"—a massive storehouse of information akin to the universe's supercomputer. These records contain a comprehensive collection of all the events, deeds, words, feelings, thoughts, and intentions that have ever occurred in the world's history. Beyond being a mere memory storehouse, the Akashic records are interactive, exerting a profound influence on our everyday lives, relationships, feelings, beliefs, and the realities we manifest.

My Past-Life Regression

I had my own powerful experience with past-life regression, and I encourage you to look into working with a professional when you are ready to have your own. In my case, I worked with an incredibly gifted guide who was with me through an energetically vibrational time—a woman named Hannah, who I met during an experience at a sweat lodge held by the Center for Peace. When I asked Hannah to do my past-life regression, she immediately scheduled one with me. I remember that day quite vividly. The driveway to my house was about a quarter of a mile long, so you could see someone pull in from the street and watch as they drove up the driveway. As I saw Hannah pull up, I knew that by the time she left, I was going to be a different person.

I did not know what to expect when she started. I lay down on a couch, nearly seven months pregnant. At this point in time, I was doing a lot of spiritual work on myself and examining the programs that I was running. In the South, it's very common for you to finish high school and then marry your high-school sweetheart and get pregnant right away, raising your kids in the town you grew up in. But I was determined to create a better life for myself and my children—and I knew I had to make space for that to happen. I hoped that by looking into the past and understanding my soul's journey, I could do just that.

Hannah explained to me that I would be the one talking throughout the regression. She prepared to hypnotize me in order to walk with me through my mind's eye. She began by having me count backward from the number twenty slowly while I rested on a comfortable couch. As I began counting backward, she began guiding me to use specific breathwork and a relaxation technique that I was unfamiliar with: holding in the breath for four solid counts from inhale to exhale. She told me that I needed to trust myself and not let my logical mind try to explain the things I didn't understand. Then she asked me to tell her a memory from when I was fifteen years old. The first memory that came to me was when my mom threw me a little birthday party at my house and my two best friends showed up. B and CeeCee and I had been friends since we were in grade school. CeeCee's mom and dad treated me like I was another member of their family. I remembered feeling happy and grateful to my mom for throwing me this party and letting me spend time with my friends. I remembered that my mom made lasagna, because that's what I always asked her to make on my birthday, and I remember it being special because my mother subscribed to the beliefs of the Jehovah's Witnesses, which means we didn't really celebrate birthdays. So, when we did anything to celebrate my birthday, it was very special.

Hannah led me back farther, asking me to remember something when I was between five and seven years old. Then she led me back even farther and asked me to remember my birth. Many people who go on past-life regressions or assisted psychedelic medicinal journeys experience the moment of their birth. They witness themselves being born, and it forever changes them. However, that's not what happened to me during my past-life regression. I skipped my entire birth and went into a big black blank space. This was a sharp contrast from the vivid memories I had been dictating to Hannah in the hypnosis state. I remember my head moving back and forth as if I couldn't see anything. Hannah asked me if there was anything that I could see in this blank space.

In response, I described what looked like an entrance to an ancient Egyptian temple. There were only two candles on each side, dimly lighting two sculpted figures that towered over the massive doorway. I spoke to Hannah about a feeling of being dwarfed by the surrounding blackness. Hannah told me I had gone into the void.

She asked me what messages I was getting, but all I could convey was that it looked like one of the figures flanking the doorway was pouring something into the darkness beyond it. Then she told me to go back even farther. This is when the blackness faded into millions of stars and I felt myself on top of a mesa. When Hannah had me describe what I was seeing there, I told her I was talking to the stars. Someone had stolen the harvest that I, the Hunter, had gathered for the tribe. I was having a very hard time accepting the fact that I had failed to provide for my community, and that they would suffer because of it. I told Hannah that I was telling the stars that the grandmother had told me I must forgive. That this was the way things were shifting to be. That I could not stop those that would come and take from me and my community, but that I could look outside of myself and into the unlimited for help. I had to forgive. I had to let go.

Hannah took me to a space that I created, where I could talk to my daughter who I was pregnant with at the time. I sat on what seemed like a Grecian bench surrounded by white pillars and grass so green it seemed electric. I remember seeing my daughter's face, curly hair, and big doe eyes. I remember exactly what she looked like under that state of hypnosis, and to this day I'm still shocked that I recognized her face from the very moment I saw her. Hannah gave me a gift of clarity and a lesson of integration that I would not have gotten if I hadn't thought out these unfamiliar avenues.

Take a Vacation at the Void

Past-life regressions can be an amazing way to get a new perspective on what is happening in your life today. Our bodies contain memory, not just from this life but from all the other incarnations we have known; so, whether we know it or not, we carry those emotions into our lives each time we are born.

One popular theory is that the water in our bodies is the vector for emotions transmuted from one life to the next. Dr. Masaru Emoto's study of the effects of emotion on water is familiar today. Doctor Emoto took multiple containers of rice and water and specifically stated different things to them over a certain amount of time. To one jar he constantly said "I love you," and to another jar he constantly said "I hate you." He then measured the molecular structure of the granules of rice and the water for each of the jars. The jar that contained the water that was told "I love you" made perfect geometric and symmetrical shapes, what is called a Fibonacci sequence. The water that was spoken to with hatred and disdain was malformed and did not create symmetrical or cohesive patterns. This has caused some to theorize that whatever happens psychologically to your ancestors can be carried down to your body generations later, transmitted through the egg in which all embryos form.

Do you ever have moments where you don't understand your feelings, emotions, or experiences? Is it possible that the traumas from our grandmother's generation can be passed down to us, and we don't even know it? A past-life regression is a non-invasive form of hypnotism that can help you unlock some secrets to your own life.

Akashic Records

The word "Akasha" comes from an ancient Sanskrit word that means "ether" or "space"—the elemental air, the fifth element where all the other elements are formed. The Akasha is where the Akashic records are held—kind of, as I always say, a spiritual Google. Just like Google, you can find anything in the Akasha. All of the infinite information in the world is at your fingertips when you go to Google's home page, and it's the same in this space: when you reach into the Akasha, you can access universal infinite wisdom throughout all space and time. However, much like the Google search bar, if you don't know specifically what you're looking for, you might just stare at the home page without knowing quite what to do. That's very much like the Akashic records—it's the site of limitless knowledge, but it's also where people get lost. Just remember that it is your birthright to access these records. Everyone can do it—not just the well-informed, skillful, or wise. It's not gate-kept. It's not like you need to have the right hardware, or be fluent in a particular language to go in. But while you absolutely can work with it all on your own, this is where many people get stuck: they become overwhelmed and never get past the home page. That's where I come in: as a reader, I know how to search, and I know how to guide other seekers.

The Akashic records hold everything: every piece of information throughout space and time since the beginning of time. You can access all possible present choices and all potential future outcomes. There are virtually limitless potential future outcomes, but that future is shaped by the choices we make right now, of which all is recorded. We all have our own court-appointed stenographers—everything we're saying and doing in every second is going into our record. This is the information that reminds us when we access the records of who we are, and why we're here, and where we came from, and what we're here to do.

If you know what you're looking for, you can access profound truths by searching the records. But there's also the option of simply sitting and channeling the Akashic records as well. Either you go in with a list of things, or you allow the records to show you everything.

If you're just learning about the records and want to try accessing yours for the first time, you may find it most useful to work with a guide to get your first reading, because this is such an important foundation for beginning to know who you really are. If you don't know who you are and where you came from and why you're here, then you don't know where you're going and how to get there. A guided reading can help you solidify your purpose as a soul, your mission, your gifts—all of it. It helps you stand in your truth. A guide will help you verify things you already know.

Essentially, what you can do by accessing the records is bring forth all the information that your subconscious soul remembers. Your conscious brain, the one born into this physical realm, doesn't know any of it. But the subconscious soul remembers, and those memories come rushing back to the frontal lobe and allow you to really hear your consciousness when you access the Akashic records. By connecting the subconscious to your consciousness in this way, you create a highway of information and allow it to flow freely. When the soul's memories are activated in the conscious, brain magic happens. It's easy for your consciousness to catch up to something your soul already knows once it gains an awareness.

It's beneficial to have a guide or a reader, because this database is so vast. It's overwhelming. It's like visiting an unknown country—you don't know where to go or what to do. But if you have someone who has been there before or knows the lay of the land, then that makes it so much more accessible. It makes it less overwhelming and easier for you to navigate and manage. Having your record read by someone, at least in the first go-around, is a good idea. Chantal, an established reader and friend of mine, noted: "When I'm with someone in the records together, my sessions are at minimum an hour and a half long—usually much longer, because I don't rush information. I've learned not to do that. When I am in with someone and we are sitting in that energy and they may not be used to it, we take the time to acclimate ourselves to it and experience it fully, and at our own pace. Sitting in this high-frequency ethereal space can be overwhelming. I record my sessions but rarely send the recording before a week has passed, because the information should be integrated first." Your physical body cannot handle the energy of the Akasha if it's not used to it—it needs to build up a tolerance. You don't want to make yourself sick. It's very possible to overdose with too much information, which can overwhelm your system.

The Akashic records are the entire vibrational footprint and record of everything that has ever happened forever through all time and space. It is not a living library, but rather it's a vibrational library that can be accessed through certain forms of meditation. My friend Chantal came to be an incredible resource.

Here are her words about working with the records:

To acclimate and improve your ability to work with the Akashic records, there are various techniques you can explore. Guided meditations are a common and accessible way to tap into these records. Through these meditations, you can raise your consciousness to a higher-dimensional frequency where the rules of time do not apply. This allows you to access information from any point in history, just as easily as if it were happening today.

During a past-life regression, you are essentially delving into a realm that is connected to the Akashic records. This fascinating concept suggests that everything has its own Akashic record, including friendships, relationships, homes, and even yourself.

As you work with the Akashic records, it's crucial to remember that they connect every soul since the beginning of creation. This interconnectedness implies that our intentions and actions have a lasting impact on the record, influencing the experiences of others as well. Therefore, it becomes imperative to be mindful of the energies we emit into the world, as our ill intentions or actions will be imprinted on this universal memory.

This reminded me that what you put out will eventually come back to you, so it is important to be your best self so you encounter the best of others. It also brought back Don Miguel Ruiz's words in *The Four*

Agreements: "Be Impeccable with Your Word & Don't Take Anything Personally." If records were a physical item in which every day a new chapter was written based on your actions and how they affected everyone around you, would you be more intentional with how you act or spend your time?

I rely on Chantal's expertise when doing my own explorations; if you would like to do this work, I recommend checking the References and Resources sections for some great sources of information, and reaching out to qualified professionals who can guide you, like Chantal.

Working with the Akashic Records

When you explore the Akashic records, there are a few things to keep in mind. First, come up with a list of questions. It's essential to stay away from yes-or-no questions, because these are not open-ended enough to get you the answers you are seeking. However, it can be difficult to parse the expansive answers you will receive, which are sometimes called "downloads." So take the time to craft questions that you feel will give you the most specific and valuable information.

It is believed that a certain vibrational frequency of being helps you translate the Akashic records. You might call these frequencies your guides or your angels—they are also referred to as masters, teachers, and loved ones. They are your guides: your spiritual team. They take your questions to the records and return with an answer that you can understand. Specific questions tend to produce measurable results, which is why you should have them on hand when you begin. Write down the answers to your questions while you communicate with the records as if you were channeling.

When you are ready to communicate with the records, find a quiet place. Once you're settled, set an intention. When you're ready to communicate with the records, you might begin to feel different or strange. This is very normal. You also may feel nothing at all. When I open my records, I get a very intense pressure on my third eye, so I will place a Lemurian crystal on my forehead to help transmute this energy. Everyone's experience is different. You may see images or lights, or you might hear voices. If you are very intuitive and your clairs are already activated, you may experience a feeling of deep knowing. Everyone has different and unique intuitive gifts, so pay attention to what shows up for you during this time.

If you know what your own calling cards are when it comes to your clairs, you will be able to decipher the messages that are coming through for you. Don't be afraid to ask for clarity if you do not understand what the message is, and always remember to close the records when you're done, which can be accomplished by visualizing yourself closing a book, placing it back on the shelf, and leaving the space where the records are held.

PART 3
Working with the Quantum

"In the unified field there is nowhere to go because you are everywhere."

—*Becoming Supernatural,* Dr. Joe Dispenza

By now, you should have an idea of what it means to work with your electromagnetic field, your neurology, and the particles around you that are the means to successful manifestations due to quantum collapse. In this section, we're going to learn more about the idea of quantum collapsing—what it is and what it is not—as well as the energetic body work that will help us prompt it more effectively. Once you have a deeper understanding of your own personal vibration, you can start working with other companions such as animals, crystals, or psychedelics. But first, to make sure you have the most optimal experience and create the reality that you want, let's investigate how energy works around us.

If you want to create something that is new in your life, whether it's a job, a home, or a relationship, you have to stop re-creating your old life with the same mindset from before. You need to get beyond the emotional charge that past events have on you. You must establish a new framework in your mind that is not based on scarcity, but that is rather based on being unlimited. When you wake up in the morning, you don't open your eyes and know how many breaths you will take that day, because a limit doesn't exist. Based on your exercise, meditation practice, or stress level, you may take fewer or more breaths, but you don't think you're going to run out of oxygen to breathe, do you? What if you applied this concept to other aspects of your life? There is an unlimited amount of money, love, friendships, nice people, etc. The more we believe there is an unlimited potential available to us, the more expansive our thoughts can be. If you are habituated to the same familiar pattern designed to give you a predictable future based solely on past experiences, you are limiting yourself. In the quantum world, you are not separate from the potentials you want, because they already exist in your space.

CHAPTER 9

QUANTUM LEAPS

The universe that we live in is three-dimensional. Through our physical senses, we experience this world. Without taste, touch, smell, hearing, and seeing, we could not experience the physical world fully. But beyond our physical reality, how can we begin to understand concepts that aren't defined by our senses, like space and time? According to astrophysics, there is an infinite amount of space. If you take a second and really feel into the infinite space around you, it is difficult to find an "end" in that space. It seems to be eternal.

Space and Time

If space has no end, does it also contain time? As we move our bodies through space, we are experiencing time. Usually, we have a thought that then creates a vision of what we want to do, after which we act on that thought. This is one way to experience time: in acting upon your thought, you have moved from one point in space to another. For example, you pick up your phone and stand up to go take it to the other room in order to put it on the charger. The thought that you needed to charge your phone created the experience of your envisioning plugging in your phone, which allowed you to get up and move through space. When you felt that you wanted to charge your phone, you realized two points of consciousness: the point at which you were sitting reading this book, and the point at which you reached the phone charger. To bridge the gap between those two points of consciousness, you moved your physical body through space, which took time. That leads us to believe that the faster you travel between two points, the shorter amount of time it would take. If you ran into the room as opposed to walking, or conversely if there was a greater physical space between the points, it would have taken a different amount of time to get from one point to the other.

Newtonian Realities

This is exactly how Newtonian physics describes the measurement of time. We all remember having to figure out how long that train was going to take to get to the station, versus the other train that left at an earlier time and had a longer distance to follow. This is a classic mathematical equation that teaches us a method of measuring time. We knew how fast the train was going; we knew the direction in which it was headed; we even knew the distance it was going to travel. So we could make a prediction as to when the train would get to the station, just like you could predict it would only take you about thirty seconds to reach your cell-phone charger. As you move from one point of consciousness to the other, you are collapsing space. And because you are collapsing space, you experience time. Still with me?

To fully understand quantum collapsing, you must understand the basics of Newtonian physics, which are based on predictable outcomes. Newtonian physics articulate the three-dimensional universe that we live in, and the matter residing in it. At the same time, you must also understand the nonphysical quantum world, which is a reality based in a multidimensional multiverse full of energy, complete unknowns, endless possibilities, and a radical shift in perception.

When we are living in a state of stress, we are trying to control the outcome of our life. This also causes us to live in a state of polarity, where we are feeling a constant sense of lack because we don't have someone, we need something, or we are frustrated because we feel we aren't reaching the goals that we feel we should have reached. In Newtonian physics, this is an example of matter trying to affect matter. Whenever we notice a separation or a lack, we then become fueled to bridge the separation and wish to find a creative space that will enable us to get the money we want, the partner we desire, the meaningful friendship, the relaxing vacation. And once you get the thing you're trying to achieve—you found a new girlfriend, you finally went on the vacation, you got the job and are making a ton of money—you'll feel secure and complete, but only because you've gotten something outside of yourself. This mindset puts us in a constant-scarcity mindset, because we don't believe that we already *are* these things: we believe they are separate from us and we have to collect them through experiences, or they come to us through someone or something else.

In simple terms, if we understand Newtonian physics as describing the physical laws of time and space in our world, where time and space seem separate, the quantum world operates differently—it shows that there's actually less distinction between time and space. The quantum model encourages us to let go of rigid beliefs and limitations, opening ourselves up to new opportunities and understanding that there's an interconnectedness in the universe that we can tap into. By being more open to quantum possibilities, we can access the vast reservoir of creative potential within us and manifest a reality that aligns with our true desires and aspirations.

Reaching the Quantum

The quantum has been described as an invisible field of energy that unifies everything material and is an expression of the laws of nature. This governs all the laws of nature within this field. This is a place where there is more time than space. This is the place where time is eternal. Anytime you've been in the meditation and you've been told to be aware of the surrounding space—the space around your eyes, the space around your body, the infinite space in front of you and behind you and around all sides of you, the space around the planet and out into the infinite universe—you have been working with the quantum.

When you experience the quantum, instead of having tunnel vision, you open the peripheral. The more information you can take in, the more you will enhance your brain function. Some studies Dr. Joe Dispenza and his team have done show that whenever we take our attention away from matter and objects, and instead focus on the information and the energy around us, our brains work together in harmony. They also noticed that hearts beat more rhythmically, and our thoughts and expressions become more coherent. This suggests that by focusing on what is beyond the physical, we are able to get beyond our body and can connect with the autonomic nervous system. This is the part of the body that restores balance, regulating cohesion among the brain, body, heart, and energy field. When we get beyond our body and activate the autonomic nervous system, that is the point at which we become connected to the unified field, or the quantum.

In the Newtonian world, mind and matter are separate. Again, in our three-dimensional physical world, space is infinite—whereas in the quantum world, time is infinite. If time is infinite, then it is not linear, meaning there is no separation between past and future. If time is infinite, then everything is happening in the eternal present. In the material world we move through space and experience time, whereas in the quantum world we move through time and experience space. So, as you move through time, you experience other dimensions, other realities, and the infinite possibilities we spoke of earlier. It's as if you were standing in a hallway that had mirrors on each side, and you could see all directions through infinite space by looking through the mirrors: all of it is happening at the present moment.

Because we see ourselves as separate from people, things, and places, time appears as linear for us. This is living in space-time. If you were living in space-time, you would experience the world with your awareness, not with your senses—everything would be one long present moment. There would be no past and no future.

Becoming Infinite

Whenever you take your awareness away from the realm of the Newtonian matter, you begin to notice the different frequencies that are carrying information around you. What would it be like, what would your life be like, if you thought there was an infinite amount of time? If you had all the time you needed, you would have infinite possibilities, and therefore be able to live many lives. If time is infinite, then more physical spaces can exist in that infinity. If we keep making more time, it makes sense that we can fit more experiences into that time. If there is infinite time and infinite space, then we are living in the realm of endless experiences and possibilities. But how do we realize this field—how do we work with this infinite-ness?

Remember, every thought you think emits a frequency, so, to move through space and time that collapses faster than you can recognize it, you must create a new thought pattern. To manifest the dream home or the dream life you want, you must get beyond the experience and emotions that keep the momentum of that in your field. To manifest the dream home or the dream life you want, you must transcend the limitations of your current experiences and emotions that might be holding you back. Often, our past experiences, negative emotions, and limiting beliefs create a momentum that keeps us stuck in a certain pattern or frequency. And if you want to create a completely new event that is unpredictable and infinite, you have to stop unconsciously thinking that the same thing that happened in the past is going to happen again. You are a part of this unified field, you are a part of this oneness, and because there is no separation, you can know that time is eternal. Everything that you want to create already exists, because your thought alone lives infinitely in the realm of all the thoughts in the quantum field.

Many of you may have already experienced the quantum field and so have already changed your hardware and programming. If you're not sure that this is what you're doing, some of these facts about your situation might sound familiar:

You're trusting in the unknown more.

You're slowing down and relaxing.

You're extremely aware of the day-to-day and have become an observer.

Embracing the metaphysical mindset and understanding the principles of quantum physics can profoundly transform your life. By recognizing the power of your thoughts, emotions, and beliefs, you can step into the role of a conscious creator and manifest the life of your dreams. Remember, the quantum model of physics shows us that the possibilities are infinite, far beyond what the Newtonian worldview limited us to believe.

QUANTUM MANIFESTATION MEDITATION

Step into the quantum field and harness the power of the universe to manifest your deepest desires with this guided meditation. Find a quiet and comfortable space where you won't be disturbed, and let's begin:

1. Sit or lie down in a relaxed position. Close your eyes and take a deep breath in through your nose, holding it for a moment, and then exhaling slowly through your mouth. Repeat this a few times, allowing your body to relax with each breath.

2. Visualize a brilliant sphere of light above your head. This radiant ball of energy represents the quantum field, containing infinite possibilities and boundless potential. Feel its presence and know that you are connected to this limitless realm of creation.

3. As you breathe deeply, imagine a beam of light descending from the sphere and entering the crown of your head. This divine energy flows gently down through your body, bathing every cell and fiber with its luminescent glow. Feel the warmth and love of this energy as it fills you from within.

4. Now visualize the life you desire, the dream home, the fulfilling career, the loving relationships, and the abundance in all aspects of your life. See yourself living these experiences as if they were happening right now. Engage all your senses—feel the textures, hear the sounds, and taste the sweetness of success.

5. Embrace the emotions that come with achieving your desires—the joy, gratitude, and fulfillment. Allow these emotions to wash over you, knowing that they amplify the frequency of your manifestations.

6. Release any doubts or fears that may surface. Surrender them to the universe, knowing that you are supported and guided on this journey of creation.

7. Now express your gratitude to the quantum field for its abundance and blessings. Thank the universe for the manifestations that are coming your way, as if they have already materialized.

8. Slowly bring your awareness back to the present moment. Take a few deep breaths, feeling the energy of the quantum field still flowing through you.

9. When you are ready, open your eyes, and carry this sense of connection and empowerment with you throughout your day.

Remember, the quantum field responds to your thoughts, feelings, and beliefs. As you continue to practice this meditation, stay open to the signs and synchronicities that come your way. Trust that the universe is working on your behalf, aligning everything to bring your dreams into reality. Get up from your meditation as if this event has already happened.

CHAPTER 10

ENERGETIC BODYWORK

W hen I first learned about Reiki, it was through a friend I met when
I lived in Knoxville, Tennessee, shortly after I turned twenty-one
years old. I grew up in the Jehovah's Witness organization, but had
a few experiences that led me to ask my mother to allow me to stop going
to the church and to stop having the brothers and sisters, as they were
called, come over to our house to study their version of the Bible with
us. I attribute a lot of my spiritual growth to my mother, because when
I asked for this at twelve years old, my wish was granted. She only had
one rule: that I could not bring anything into the house that was "of the
Devil." That meant tarot cards, books about astrology, or anything that
the church said was of man or the world (which therefore meant it was
of the Devil). So I would go to school and to the local library to read
about the things I wasn't really allowed to read about at home. In my
nearly ten years of study, I didn't come across Reiki. I was very familiar
with other types of energetic bodywork, such as acupuncture, tapping,
and manifestation—but never Reiki.

I remember the day so clearly: I went over to my friend's home. I had
never met her before—her name was Colleen, or CeCe for short. Her

house was in a historic part of the city and was over a hundred years old. I remember that the home held a very specific type of energy, one that almost felt like sorrow. It may have been because at some point, Catholic nuns had used the building, and there were stories about traumatic things that had happened within its walls. Not only did people gossip who remembered those days or had heard of them—anyone with intuitive abilities could easily pick up on that energy. One day, my eighteen-month-old son turned to CeCe and said, "Did you see that ghost?" That kind of thing happened on a regular basis. In essence, CeCe's house was very much like an energetic portal where many people were drawn for different aspects of healing. At one point, her home had been used as a Catholic school and then sat abandoned for a very long time. There was a sense of unease and a restless energy around the home: what once had been a thriving part of Knoxville, Tennessee, had become a less-than-desirable area of town with crime and violence around every corner. Cece's home seemed to act as a border, and many people were drawn to her home to work creatively together in the forms of art, music, and yoga. I was drawn to CeCe to get my first Reiki treatment and to become a teacher myself, although I did not know that until I received my first treatment.

I remember that day vividly—the entire experience was so intense, culminating in a moment when I felt I could see a bright orange light emanating from behind my eyes as CeCe worked on my body and gave me Reiki. When I opened my eyes, the room was filled with the same orange glow. I wasn't able to tell the difference between what I was seeing with my eyes closed versus open. It was like I was in a chamber in a sensory-deprivation tank that was specifically tuned to the color therapy that I needed. Orange bathed the entire room, and, as my eyes adjusted, I realized that the color of the room wasn't changing. As I looked out the window, I noticed how orange the sky was. I kept my hands close to my womb, resting right above my first chakra. I was experiencing a deep sadness about my first-born child and the weight of becoming a single mother. I felt called to hold my hands over my womb and send myself love.

I had come to this Reiki session with CeCe without a lot of prior knowledge or expectations. I hadn't really started in-depth spiritual work and was solely learning from books and other teachers. I was open to whatever resonated with me. But when CeCe came into the picture, some-thing shifted. What she shared with me after that first Reiki session were things she couldn't possibly have known because I hadn't told her. She spoke with me and had a diagram of my body printed out on a sheet of paper, on which were colors and circles on various parts of my body. She told me my second chakra was overperforming, causing her to see a bright orange hue around me. Once I got up from the table after that first Reiki session, I knew I wanted to help other people feel the way I had just been helped. I decided to learn how to transmute the energies that directly affect our bodies from our experiences. From there, I started div-ing deeper into psychological theories that correlate with the formation of the chakras in the body. For some of the resources that helped me most, please take a look at page TK. Just like my own transformative experience with Reiki, a single moment of realization can set you on a path of pro-found growth and understanding. If any of the practices and concepts that

I share in this chapter resonate deeply with you, consider delving further into their study. Whether it's exploring the Akashic records, working with past-life regression, or embracing the art of alchemy, continued learning and practice will empower you to access the quantum field and unlock the hidden treasures of the universe. Your journey to a metaphysical mindset has only just begun; as you delve deeper into the mysteries of existence, you'll uncover the brilliance of your true potential.

Reiki

Many people consider Reiki a pseudoscience, even though many modernized Western institutions recognize it for healing. The Cleveland Clinic links directly to an appointment page on which you can schedule Reiki consultations and get an appointment with approved specialists through their website. According to the National Center for Complementary and Alternative Medicine, Reiki can be used for stress reduction and more. Today, the number one leading cause of death in the United States is heart disease, and stress is a primary risk factor. Even for those who doubt the science behind Reiki, the fact is that it's a non-invasive way to reduce stress. Reiki is derived from the Japanese words "rei," meaning "universal life," and "ki," which is a word for the vital life force energy that flows through all living things. Therefore, Reiki is the universal energy that flows through all living things. Anyone can tap into the energy of Reiki at any point in time, under any circumstances.

During my first Reiki session, I was not under the certain impression that I was going to have a life-changing experience. All I knew was that for seventy-two hours before my session, CeCe suggested that I abstain from caffeine and any red meat, and she recommended that I meditate and conserve my energy as much as possible. This was in order for me to be in a certain energetic frequency to receive the Reiki treatment I was going to undergo. In Reiki, the practitioner is a channel between the person who is receiving the treatment and the universal life-force energy that flows through everything. This universal energy can also flow through the practitioner's energy field, through their hands, and to the client. The practitioner is not creating the energy; it does not come from the practitioner. They are merely a vessel that the energy can move through. There are reports that a Reiki practitioner does not become drained by this process; but if certain steps aren't taken, there is a risk of a client leaving energetic baggage behind on the practitioner. Many cultures believe that the palms of the hands contain their own chakras. Reiki initiates and opens the palm chakras with a certain specific symbolism that is only used or called on for Reiki sessions.

Reiki sessions can last anywhere from about sixty to ninety minutes. The Reiki practitioner will gently place their hands, palm-down, on the person's body, or hover them above it at a specific energetic location. Each practitioner feels energy differently, so the sensations that they feel throughout the body can show up in different ways, which dictate how long the practitioner will stay on that part of the body. Reiki is not specific to any type of disease or condition. There is a list of medical organizations that offer Reiki in the United States.

Unlike yoga or other healing arts, Reiki is passed down from a teacher to a student through what is called attunement. Attunement allows the student to connect to the universal energy. The student becomes the vessel of Reiki and is then able to move Reiki energy, first within themselves and then throughout the bodies of others. The first attunement for Reiki consists of moving energy within the self. Once you have mastered the energy of the self, you can move on to helping others move energy as well. Before Reiki became popular, the symbols that enabled these practices were held tightly within the organizations that comprised the Reiki masters.

Once the Internet became what it has become, and especially in the age of social media, the symbols for Reiki became more universally distributed. This created a shift in how the energy was passed down between masters. Now people can access the symbols without an attunement. This is almost like being given a car before you know how to drive it. Until a teacher has attuned you to channel the energy of Reiki, you are not truly practicing the energetic movement.

In the first attunement, each student gets three symbols representing aspects of power, emotional and mental balance, and distance healing. Each student receives three attunements to these three symbols four separate times; with each repetition, the connection and frequency deepens. The next attunements, from level 2 on to master, are similar, but they all involve different symbols, because each represents a different energetic pathway. Receiving a regular attunement can be a powerful experience. For me, it was what propelled me to find my purpose spiritually. The energetic pathways are opened by a Reiki master, which allows energy to flow freely through your body and affect your health and the health of others. For me, I experienced this when the orange light I had sensed during my first session reappeared with the same warmth and what felt like a fiery tingle—almost like my entire body was asleep. Once you have the attunement, the effects can range from a heightened intuitive awareness to an enhanced psychic sensitivity. You can experience anything from a heightened knowing of when someone specific is about to reach out to you, to seemingly having an idea that creates a new avenue of financial opportunity drop into your head out of nowhere.

The distance-healing symbol is the last symbol that is taught in the Reiki level 2 training. The symbol is perhaps one of the most useful of the three you first acquire, because it enables healing energy to be sent to someone who is not physically with the client. Because this is a universal energy that can move about freely and isn't controlled, but is guided and channeled, this energy can be sent to yourself in the past and in the future. The symbol itself means existing outside the concepts of present, past, or future, meaning it's essentially not bound by the Newtonian view and is used for sending healing across time and space.

When you want to send Reiki to the past, it is not in order to change something that has already happened—because you cannot simply change the past. When Reiki is sent to the past, it can heal the emotions or the pain and the damage that remain in the present moment. What we attempt to do when we send Reiki to the past is to reframe the experience so that we can learn from it. You can send it to release the pain, the guilt, the shame, or the judgment you felt in that moment, and move on with your life. Reiki offers alternative choices when it comes to experiences you have already had, including choosing not to continue to give time and energy to people who cast judgment and have unrealistic expectations.

One very important thing to remember is that Reiki cannot be used to change people or to change the behaviors they have exhibited in the past. That has to be their own choice. What you can do is send Reiki to people for the highest good. When you do that, whatever happens is not up to you. When you are channeling Reiki, you can't control where the Reiki goes or what it addresses during that session. Reiki is the wisdom that knows what is best for each person and acts accordingly.

If you feel called to Reiki, please check out the list of resources in the back of the book. I've listed some material that was most useful to me, including more in-depth explanations of symbols and how to get started if you wish to have a session or eventually become a master yourself.

EFT Tapping

Emotional Freedom Technique (EFT) is self-help practice that involves tapping on specific points of the body with the fingers while focusing on a particular emotion or problem. It's like dancing: it can make you feel good because it's a way to release and process emotions. In the same way, EFT tapping is a physical way to release and reduce stress. The principles of EFT draw on the traditional Chinese medicine practice of acupuncture. Key acupressure points on the hands, face, and body are tapped with fingertips while focusing on uncomfortable feelings or concerns. Positive affirmations are then used to neutralize those feelings.

Affirmations used in EFT are usually statements along the lines of something like "Even though I have this [name of issue], I deeply love and completely accept myself. I forgive myself as best I can. I want to get to a calm and peaceful place." For optimal results, you should be hyper-specific: this is a time to focus on the negative, because you are setting yourself up to transmute that energy. Spend time identifying the issue that you will be releasing.

Simply state the problem, and be as detailed as you can. Why is this a problem for you? Measure your level of discomfort surrounding the issue on a scale of zero to ten, with ten being the worst and zero being a situation in which there's no problem at all. When you're ready, say the setup statements out loud: "Even though I have this [name of condition], I still deeply love and completely accept myself." Say this while continually tapping on your hand with your fingertips. Tap through the points while you're speaking about the problem, letting yourself get all the inner voices out. Key tapping points start at the top of the head, the eyebrow, beside the eye, below the eye, above the lip, the chin, the collarbone, the under-arm, and on the side of the wrist. If you feel called to work on a specific space, such as your upper lip or beside the eye, focus on that space and energy, because you may need to focus on one area over others. It's basically acupuncture without the needles.

In the *Law of Attraction* books by Esther Hicks, she describes a practice called a "gratitude rampage." Essentially, it entails a stream-of-consciousness recitation of all of the things you are grateful for. This is kind of like the opposite: instead of a gratitude rampage, it's more of a negativity rampage. Name everything you have a problem with, whether that's your lack of accountability, issues with monogamy, your issues with money—whatever it may be. Then ask yourself what the worst thing is about this problem. What are the feelings that are associated with it? Get it all out, and tap through the points.

I taught an EFT workshop at a great music festival here in California called Lightning in a Bottle. During my EFT Workshop at Lightning in a Bottle in 2023, a woman came in who had had a traumatic brain injury, followed by multiple brain surgeries, which left her with permanent brain damage. She shared her story during my workshop, and it truly was inspirational. She practiced EFT tapping after her traumatic brain injury and surgeries, and it was one of the few tools that helped her to have a better understanding and to neutralize feelings of despair.

Noemi, a psychedelic-assisted therapy practitioner, describes EFT tapping like this:

> The way I describe tapping when I'm in more of a group environment where I don't know who knows what is that it is one of those techniques that helps to regulate the nervous system by releasing emotion and relaxing the body. And so it works as a type of acupressure plus exposure therapy that helps us feel our feelings and accept them in order to release old ties to situations that caused unresolved emotions to get stuck in our nervous system. This is a way to go back and release latent stress and emotions from the body.

When I sit with people, we talk about where they're holding on to emotion in the body and by awareness practices. When you talk about the fear, even little things prompt an emotional response that we feel in our bodies. That means that something is stored there. Fear is a signal of where we are holding on to emotion in the body. When we're in a Zoom meeting, we're probably not in a state of danger, and yet our bodies are telling us that we need to be in that fight-or-flight, even though nothing is actually prompting that response except our thoughts: how we are feeling the majority of the time due to modern society and constant stresses. We might feel fear without an immediate physical reason for it, but whatever made us feel that way is a trigger for something else. Just notice what your body is holding on to that isn't helpful to you in a given situation.

There aren't really any prerequisites to learning how to practice these techniques. You just need to be willing to feel your feelings and be willing to accept what is going on there. And potentially, you need to be willing to feel differently, even if it happens slowly and over time. Even the thought of wanting to do it starts a new set of neurons firing, which creates a new pathway—this may not feel like much, but it is a start.

So, let's pause for a minute. Feeling your feelings. That's a big one for a lot of us. Our modern society has told us to not be emotional. This doesn't benefit us in the long run. How do you feel about feeling your feelings?

So many of us have not been taught how to express negative emotion, or have been limited to only sadness and anger, leaving our understanding of more nuanced emotions underdeveloped. As a result, those emotions get stuck in our bodies. It's crucially important to have a caregiver when we're around the age of six who will help us regulate our brain waves while they are still absorbing everything around us. That person should be there to help us learn how to express emotion safely. If you didn't have that experience, then as an adult you're less likely to know how to do it. In that case, you might revert to childlike coping mechanisms to help you feel safe.

If you're noticing an intensity to energy in certain areas of your body, then it is worthwhile to focus on that area for a little while longer. If you are working with a guide, they can use specific points for your anxiety or stress release. The ten points I usually use are organs that tend to hold specific emotions—for example, the gallbladder point is located next to the eye. According to traditional Chinese medicine, the gallbladder holds feelings of frustration and anger. Knowledge about acupressure points in traditional Chinese medicine goes back thousands of years. It hasn't been until recently that we've been able to actually measure what happens on an energetic level when we use these points. The energetic charge can be measured with a device called a galvanometer, which not only can detect the precise locations of acupressure points, but also can help determine energy buildup in certain areas by measuring the electrical resistance of skin.

If you are hoping to work through issues like major anxiety, depression, or PTSD, it's best to be guided by someone certified in clinical EFT. While EFT clinicians will not diagnose or offer any prescriptions, they have been put through a process that gives them the knowledge to work with people who have trauma, and they can assist you with the side effects and symptoms of living with mental illness.

Noemi, who is certified in clinical EFT, puts it this way: clinical EFT is about "focusing first on what's happening here in our bodies right now and then accepting that in order to release it and allow rest. . . . It's not about re-experiencing the old stuff or lingering in it, it's about giving yourself permission to feel what is here with you right now, and that can be very gentle and graceful." Basically, it can help you deal with what you currently have so that you can create space for new things, like manifestations. You must clear out the past in order to be able to move forward and realize your manifestations.

EFT was first studied with war veterans, and they saw such great results that they tried to offer this in the Department of Veterans Affairs. Unfortunately, the VA said no. There's still some pushback against EFT, but more and more organizations are working with it as complementary medicine.

An EFT Experience

The following is the story of one of Noemi's patients. It's just one example of the amazing benefits that can come from opening yourself up to a metaphysical practice that treats the body and mind in a holistic way.

I have had depression and anxiety for as long as I can remember. I have been on medication since I was fifteen or sixteen years old. I spent years in therapy, graduated from it, went back, and graduated again.

I figured this was my path in life, that this was "living." I knew what I was "supposed" to do, how I was "supposed" to help myself. And yet living it was so elusive—I felt like I was missing something, some tool to help me make it all connect.

I was on a girls' trip in Joshua Tree which Noemi was also attending.

We had already been there for a day and were flying high on more than just our emotions. The previous night we all took a microdose, and I am pretty sure we saw aliens.

Over the weekend, anytime someone got even the slightest tinge of sadness, we called over Noemi and she took the sadness away. EVERY. TIME. Over the course of the weekend, I watched her hold space for woman after woman, lifting them up and reminding them of their power. I gave in; I had to know the secret. I asked Noemi, "How? How is it you can hold space for all these people and take none of the pain on yourself?"

She asked if I really wanted to know the answer. What kind of question was that? *Do I really want to know?* Did I not just ask the question?

She pulled me in closer; she answered almost in a whisper.

"None of it matters."

"None of it matters?" I repeated to her.

"None of it matters, it's all just our perception and what we allow."

MIND BLOWN. She explained that everything I had felt and was experiencing was because of the past, because of emotions that I had held on to which were now affecting me in the present.

Now, I had heard of the idea of generational trauma before. As a granddaughter of Holocaust survivors, I knew that my DNA had been fundamentally changed because of their experiences—but had no idea how to deal with such a thing. Noemi invited me to tap with her.

We started with how I could learn to forgive myself. Right before COVID, I had discovered that I had a thirty-centimeter, twelve-pound fibroid in my stomach. My only indicator at the time was heartburn, and again being a German Jew grandchild of the Holocaust. Noemi and I tapped on my anxiety, my guilt, this belief that I had somehow caused this fibroid and deserved it. I have always had the twisted belief that when bad things happen to me, I deserve it—that I was the reason for the bad.

In that moment, Alex realized that she had been carrying these burdens for far too long. She had allowed her past experiences and negative beliefs to define her present and dictate her future. But now, as Noemi helped her tap them away, a sense of liberation washed over her.

As they continued tapping, Alex's mind became clearer, and she started to see that she was not to blame for the fibroid or any of the other misfortunes in her life. She recognized that she deserved happiness and peace, just like anyone else.

With each tap, Alex shed layers of self-doubt and negativity, feeling lighter and more empowered. Noemi's guidance and the tapping technique had opened her eyes to a new perspective. She realized that she had the power to let go of limiting beliefs and create a more positive and fulfilling life.

In that transformative moment, Alex felt a renewed sense of hope and determination. She knew that she still had work to do, but she now had the tools to navigate her journey toward healing and self-acceptance.

As the session came to an end, Alex thanked Noemi for her incredible insight and guidance. She left that day with a newfound sense of clarity and self-belief. From that point forward, Alex vowed to continue tapping into her inner strength, letting go of the past and embracing the possibility of a brighter future.

> EFT allowed me to let that guilt go. To let go of the belief that bad things happen because I am a bad person. I could realize that the pain and guilt were all left over from the past, and that I was suddenly projected into the future. I really was creating my pain, but it had nothing to do with me being a bad person. I just held on to bad feelings.
>
> I tap daily; I make sure that I keep the energy inside me moving and flowing so I do not become stuck in the past.

CHAPTER 11

HEALING BEYOND BOUNDARIES

The term "somatic" means "relating to the body." While both somatic therapy and energetic bodywork recognize the interconnectedness of the mind and body, somatic therapy primarily focuses on the body as a gateway to healing emotional and psychological issues. It works directly with bodily sensations and movements to release trauma and promote self-awareness. Energetic bodywork, on the other hand, works with the body's energy system to restore balance and promote overall well-being. A somatic therapist uses metaphysical techniques to release trauma trapped in your body. As we've discussed in earlier chapters, these low-vibration thoughts and emotions can stay in the body and cause a number of issues.

Ecstatic dance, intense breathwork, yoga—these things are part of the somatic therapist's toolbox. There are many techniques that a somatic therapist can use to help someone release trauma from the body. A few of the most common ones are:

Sequencing: This technique involves paying very close attention to the sensations in your body as tension rises during stress and then dissipates—for example, if you feel your heart race fast, and then a lump forms in your throat.

Titration: Titration is a gradual process that involves experiencing incremental levels of distress, aiming to effectively release and alleviate tension from the body. During titration, you observe the changes in your body as a therapist takes you through a traumatic memory. If you feel physical sensations, you will be asked to let the therapist know what and where those are. This is also extremely helpful if you are using somatic therapy as a tool before you go into deeper therapies such as Reiki or plan to use psychedelics with a clinical or trained guide.

Resourcing: Resourcing is almost like creating a vision board. It involves recalling the things that help you feel safe, remind you of your best attributes, and affirm what you want in a relationship. This information is established to provide a sense of calm for you as an emotional anchor. Resourcing means collecting the things that make you feel good and imagining your bliss.

Pendulation: This therapeutic technique is like past-life regression. A therapist leads you through the past and to the traumatic experience you are hoping to get past; but unlike in past-life regression, the goal is to release the energy from that experience.

Grounding: Grounding is the act of connecting foundationally to the Earth and sensing your body through the ground. This has been shown to calm the nervous system and is a foundational technique in most metaphysical practices.

Body Awareness: Similar to the first attunement in Reiki, this practice teaches that the first step in learning to release tension from the body is in identifying where it is located. One of the first things that a somatic therapist will work on with someone who is trying to release trauma is body awareness.

Hakomi: This is a type of somatic therapy that is centered on mindfulness and the ability to stay in the present moment, with no expectation and no judgment. The therapist will provide an atmosphere that is holding the space for acceptance, which helps your body identify programs you were running unconsciously. By accessing this unconscious material, a therapist can help you safely release it.

Sensory therapy combines techniques from neuroscience and the Hakomi method, attachment theory, psychotherapy, and somatic therapy all into one extremely powerful therapy. Sensory therapy helps people re-experience an event and then physically act in a favorable way. For example, the victim of an assault will experience being able to escape. Someone grieving a traumatic loss will physically feel that they did not lose their loved one in such a traumatic way. This is somewhat like an inner-child work experience where you go back to a period of your life in which you did not get what you needed and provide it for yourself.

Neurosomatic therapy identifies tension and pain in the nervous system, the skeletal system, and the soft tissue. Massage and yoga are techniques that are mainly used in neurosomatic therapy.

EMDR therapy: So-called Eye Movement Desensitization and Reprocessing facilitates the processing of traumatic memories and other life experiences. During EMDR sessions you become aware of emotionally upsetting experiences in microdoses while focusing on an external stimulus. The therapist will direct lateral eye movements that allow you to access the traumatic memories so that new associations can be formed and more adaptive memories can take their place. One focus is on the concept that an emotional wound can fester and cause intense suffering. The belief is that once the wound is removed, healing can continue.

Somatic Experiencing by Dr. Peter A. Levine: Sometimes referred to as SE, this practice is a way of engaging with the feeling of a traumatic event and then safely releasing the energy associated with it. In some instances, your therapist will ask you to talk about your traumatic experience, while others might ask you to describe the physical sensations that you felt during the experience. Sometimes you are asked to move your body in a way that activates those feelings. In each case, the therapist will engage you to release that built-up energy safely so that you can expel it from your body. In somatic therapy, touch is key, because our instinct is to touch our body whenever we feel pain or trauma. When we experience pain or trauma, our instinct is to touch the affected area. For example, if you cut your arm, the first thing you do is grab it with your other hand. Similarly, in somatic therapy, touch is used to facilitate the release of trapped energy and emotions. The therapist may gently touch certain areas of your body or guide you in self-touch exercises. By engaging the body through touch, somatic therapy aims to address and release tension, trauma, and negative emotions that are stored in the body.

Sound Healing

Sound healing combined with somatic therapy is becoming increasingly popular. The body and brain respond to sound waves. Sound healing capitalizes on that connection, using noise and vibration to target certain areas of the body in order to decrease stress, trauma, or pain. The therapist sends sound waves into the client's body using different techniques. Instruments may be used, including singing bowls, tuning forks, and gongs, all of which directly affect the body where there is pain, tension, or trauma. Singing or chanting is also a way to use different healing frequencies to achieve similar effects. Allowing clients to produce their own sounds as they work through the experience is also a powerful method.

Sound has been deeply revered since ancient times as a sacred property, capable of producing elevated emotions and even physical effects. The variety of sound tools that have been found in ancient civilizations is beyond extensive. Today, we have a growing body of research that backs up the idea that sound can heal. Studies have shown that vibrational forces of sound are both audible and inaudible to the human senses. Sound waves emit a constant vibration that we are sometimes not aware of. These waves wash over us every minute, every hour of every day, and they continue to send out vibrations endlessly into infinite space and time. Sound vibrations can also penetrate our physical bodies. This has been suggested as a way to improve metabolism, stimulate tissue, and even improve blood circulation.

Different neurological studies have proven that listening to music makes us more creative and allows us to relieve stress and improve our moods. This is because when we listen to music, our brains become flooded with the chemical dopamine. It also releases oxytocin, which is the hormone that allows us to bond to others. In 2006, a study by the *Journal of Advanced Nursing* found that those who listen to music feel less pain and experience less anxiety than those who do not.

The effects of sound healing have been documented, and it has been shown to improve or even cure some ailments such as stress, PTSD, pain, and depression.

I know for a fact that one of my great friends who struggles with depression uses Taylor Swift as her sound healing. She will play binaural beats on one computer and Taylor on her phone, and that helps her feel better. The key is using music that will place you in a higher state.

That could be anything, as long as it helps you feel better. Sound healing doesn't have to include Tibetan bowls or giant gongs or somebody playing a tuning bowl. Sound healing can be whatever resonates with your body and helps you produce that flood of dopamine.

Another way to create a similar effect is referred to as the Bonnie method, which involves guided imagery used in conjunction with music. Think of it like making a music video to your favorite song that's just images of your life, including pictures of experiences that you want to happen. The Bonnie method is kind of like creating a digital vision board. Align it with a sound that elicits a certain level of emotion for you, and watch it every day to see results.

The Dalcroze method teaches music to students as therapy. If you are a teacher and you focus on rhythm as an expression of learning, this might be a method that you are called to as a student. It helps increase awareness, significantly elevating cognitive function.

One of the most common methods of sound healing is mantra, or guided, meditation. If you are someone who can't sit in front of your computer watching a yoga session without feeling disconnected, consider a practice that incorporates sound healing in this way. Kundalini Yoga incorporates singing and chanting meditations, which can really propel your experience.

Neurological Music Therapy (NMT) proposes that the creation and enjoyment of music has a positive influence on the brain. It has been especially helpful in the treatment of stroke victims who have aphasia, or loss of language—Senator Gabby Giffords integrated NMT into her recovery program after her gunshot injury to the head in 2011. NMT is a specialized form of therapy that utilizes music to address cognitive, emotional, sensory, and motor-function issues caused by neurological conditions or disorders. Unlike other music-related therapies, NMT is specifically tailored to target the brain's neuroplasticity—the brain's ability to reorganize and form new neural connections in response to learning, experience, and injury.

Root Frequency Entrainment (RFE) is based on the premise that our souls emit a specific frequency when operating at their optimal capacity. This practice centers around aligning ourselves with that fundamental frequency. It suggests that we are out of balance, because of the stress, anxiety, and chaos that we encounter in our physical world. In our daily lives, we are drawn to interact with frequencies and vibrational points that are familiar to our soul. This might be why you're drawn to certain music or places—it's because your soul has a memory attached to those frequencies. Remember when we talked about the Akashic records and how your subconscious holds your memories? Root Frequency Entrainment centers on this. If you feel called, maybe Akashic record readings in conjunction with Root Frequency Entrainment would be a way for you to explore sound healing.

There is also tuning fork therapy. This method employs a tuning fork, a metal instrument with two prongs that emits one specific acoustic frequency (typically A 440) after being tapped on a hard surface, whether a body part (like your knee), a piece of furniture, or by a crystal. Personally I've always got a tuning fork in my bag—it's gotten me pulled aside at the airport multiple times. It's probably one of my favorite tools for body and soul synching, because tuning forks allow your vibrational frequency to come into another frequency, all by just striking the tuning fork.

Probably the most popular therapy in sound healing is singing bowls. These have been used in Asia dating back as far as the twelfth century. Their sound helps produce a sense of calm and repairs the mind, allowing your body to reduce stress and lower blood pressure. Their vibrational frequencies are also said to improve circulation.

There's also vibroacoustic therapy. This is a therapy in which sound is directly applied to the body. So, in a typical session, you lie down on a special bed onto which speakers have been installed so that sounds and vibrations penetrate on a cellular level. Vibroacoustic therapy helps patients recover from strokes and serious injuries. In 2018, I was asked to come to an event in California in which I used a device in order to listen to the sound of some plants. During this activation, I attached gaming chairs (like what someone sits in to play video games) to this device, then played the music from the plants directly into the chairs. Not only could you hear the music from the plants, you could feel it and experience it.

Different instruments are used for sound healing, including the voice. Originally there was a twelve-note annotation scale, which was discovered by a Gregorian monk named Guido de Arezzo. Guido knew that the monks could have metaphysical experiences when they sang in certain ways. Tibetan throat singing is another practice that is a form of using the voice as a musical instrument. It involves multiphonic (two-toned) chanting in a low tone called a *jok-kay* overlapping a high tone called a *bar-da*. Singing in multiple tones makes it sound like the singers are reaching multiple octaves. Certain groups of monks have used this technique as a meditative practice.

Instruments Used in Sound Healing

Didgeridoo: used in meditation to heal and unblock energy within the body. The use of this instrument originated in Australia as an indigenous practice some 1500 years ago. The original purpose was ceremonial. However, in 2005, the British medical journal discovered that playing the didgeridoo actually helped reduce sleep apnea, because it strengthened the muscles in the upper airway. It also improved the symptoms of asthma.

Djembe: originated in West Africa, a djembe is a wooden drum that is dressed in goat hide and ropes. It is typically used to alter consciousness by inducing trance states. It is said to reduce stress and to calm the spirit. Its use is very common in drumming circles and in meditation practices.

Gong: one of my favorite instruments to use in sound healing. I have produced a specific gong meditation with a talented musician named Mike Dillon for a music festival called Jam Cruise—the gong is one of my absolute favorite ways to fall into the infinite space-time. Not only does it induce an incredible meditative state, it can actually ease physical, emotional, and spiritual pain.

Native American flute: produces a soothing sound that reduces blood pressure and eases anxiety and depression.

Rain sticks: Provide relaxation and a sense of calm with the sound of falling rain. Traditionally made from dried-out cactuses filled with small stones and seeds.

Wind chimes: Enhance the flow of life force and carry an elemental power. Popular in Feng Shui and require wind to create music.

PART 4
The Companion Kingdoms

"When you begin to work with birds and receive from them, the mysteries of both the Earth and the Heavens open to you."

—Ted Andrews, *Animal Speak*

This planet can be categorized into five main kingdoms as defined by biology: animal, plant, fungi, protist, and monera. Humans are just a part of the animal kingdom. In this last chapter, we are going to dive deep into working with the other elements of our planet: the stones, the animals, the plants, the herbs, and, yes, the mushrooms.

Starting with a chapter on animal energy, I'm going to tell you how spirit guides may appear as animals. Then we will move on to the ancient technology of crystals, including the neural network of the planet, as well as the use of plant spirits as medicinal companions. In order to share this chapter with full transparency, I have to give you a little more of a background on why I became someone that worked with the plant spirit community.

If you are familiar with my *Metaphysical Cannabis Oracle Deck*, you probably know a bit of my backstory. For those of you who don't, let me tell you the story: I did not have the typical life that many young women in America have.

I was adopted at a very young age by a woman who I would later find out was not just a friend of my mother's, but actually her girlfriend. I was raised in a queer household when being queer was extremely dangerous. I grew up knowing very well that love is love, that who you choose to love is your own business and no one should have a say over that. It wasn't until my adoptive mother passed away that I learned that she had actually been in a relationship with my *biological* mother. And it wasn't until I started working deeply with psychedelics that I learned how to integrate and come to terms with the life I had lived and the life I felt had been taken from me.

I was not a girl who was popular in high school; I was not someone who even wanted a superlative. My entire high school career revolved around singing in the choir, dancing competitively on the dance team, and being constantly reminded that I was unlike most of the people in the school. My mother was significantly older, and her health was declining fast. If I had known at fifteen that I would only have ten more years with her, I'm sure I would have lived a different life.

I grew up in a tiny town of less than three thousand people, and my entire graduating class was less than 190 people. I can say positively that I am the only one from the class who is now an outspoken cannabis and psychedelic advocate, even though many of the people who were the first ones to introduce me to psychedelics are still in the town. Some became teachers and are actively hiding their closeted medicine journeys, too. The first time I ever did anything psychedelic, I was in a small town in North Carolina named Black Mountain, which sits about thirty minutes outside Asheville. They welcomed me into a community of people that celebrated weekly by getting together and enjoying psychedelics while creating music. It felt like something out of a cult, but not in the cold way that I was used to, having grown up with the Jehovah's Witnesses. This felt like one of those hippie cults that you would read about from the seventies. And in actuality it wasn't a cult at all: it was a group of people who knew how much creativity could be sparked with an intentional companion such as a psychedelic.

After getting locked in a bathroom for a good five minutes and needing my friend to come and get me, the entire night made me reevaluate how I was living my life. I went back that weekend and wrote one of the most powerful essays I had ever written for the college professor teaching my speech class. Doctor Love—yes, that was his real name—was a cancer survivor who had used cannabis to help him heal. In 2010 in southeast Tennessee, using cannabis to heal your cancer was not something you could talk about and really be taken seriously. It was after this trip to Black Mountain that I became more of an advocate for psychedelics and decided to pursue a path that I felt needed to be talked about in my community.

The first companion that I ever worked with was not cannabis but psilocybin, or mushrooms. I was raised to believe that I was allergic to cannabis, to deter me from partaking after my brother was arrested for smoking a joint in an abandoned building. I had been adopted into a white family by proxy and was the only colored child they had. When I was twelve and my brother was seventeen, he was arrested as just described. He got off with community service and a slap on the wrist. My mother—who was very self-aware and knew that the society we lived in can be unfair to people of color, and specifically in small towns—told me I was allergic to cannabis so that I would not smoke it. So I reasoned that if I was allergic to cannabis, then I couldn't possibly be allergic to mushrooms, right? As a result, the first psychedelic companion that I sat with was psilocybin.

If it wasn't for the guided and integrative sessions that I had with psilocybin throughout this past decade, I don't believe I would have been able to cope with all the things that I had to deal with growing up, from my aunt being murdered, to my brother moving out, to my mom's health quickly declining, after which she went on hospice. It's these companions in the plant-spirit realm, along with my human companions, that have helped me move through some of the harder things in my life.

Over these past two decades where I have specifically been doing this work with the metaphysical, I feel like I've been building up a little toolbox, and that toolbox is what I'm sharing with you here in this book. This chapter will not cover every in-depth aspect about the companion kingdoms—about animal energy, about crystals, about plant-spirit medicine, or about psychedelics. This is just an introduction for those of you who want to dive deeper into learning about how your own magic can be amplified.

Remember that the universe is saying to you: be grateful and I'll give you something to be grateful about. Explore some of those ways that the universe is showing you gratitude in a language that you may not understand yet. The universe doesn't hear what you say—but it does see and feel what you put out.

CHAPTER 12

ANIMAL ENERGY

A nimal energy surrounds us. In my case, I hear the birds as soon as I wake up: I know the sound of the mourning doves in the front yard; I know the sound of the crows and the ravens when they're out on the street in my neighborhood. In my home, I will never forget the pitter-patter of our little dog Lola's nails scratching across the floor in her old age. And I know if I walk down certain streets in my neighborhood, I will encounter certain cats that I've developed a companionship with.

The natural world is full of symbols that are crying out for recognition every day. And for those who have opened themselves up to a metaphysical mindset, there are so many powerful ways to understand them. Throughout history, dating back to ancient times, humans have recognized the profound connection between the natural world and a higher power. The ancients understood that visible bodies in nature are symbolic representations of invisible forces, and they revered these lower kingdoms of nature as a way to worship the divine. By studying living things and the wonders of animate and inanimate nature, the sages of old gained insight into the intelligence and power of the Eternal One. It gave them insight and the ability to foretell events based on their behavior and patterns.

By recognizing the divine presence in all aspects of nature, we open ourselves up to a deeper understanding of the universe and its mysteries. Connecting with the natural world allows us to tap into the higher realms of consciousness and spiritual awareness. Just as the ancients found divine inspiration in the wonders of nature, we too can find spiritual insights and guidance by embracing the beauty and wisdom of the natural world.

A quote from author Manly P. Hall's *The Secret Teachings of All Ages* states it best:

> Humanity has always recognized that it is a part of nature and that nature is a part of humanity. Priestesses and shamans were tied to the rhythms of the planet, and they could decipher natural messages in order to help other people remember the animals will speak to those who listen and that the trees themselves are divine. Different societies expressed their understanding of nature in a variety of ways, but those varied philosophies and cosmologies often aligned with almost eerie accuracy to the Law of Correspondence: as above, so below. All things are connected and have significance. We cannot separate the spiritual from the physical or the visible from the invisible because these principles are the paradox of nature.

Studying animal totems means understanding how the spiritual is manifesting into the natural world. A totem can be anything: it could be an animal, a different kind of being, or an energy that is associated with you during your life such as non-animal spirits. Maybe you see a mythical phoenix or Pegasus—these aren't real animals but contain an energy and mysticism that can help you. These are all archetypes that have their own qualities and characteristics that are reflected through expressions of nature. The characteristics and abilities of these totems will tell you about your own powers and intuitive abilities. When you come across an animal and learn about it, you merge your energetic field with this archetype energy, which can help you understand the experiences in your life. Even if an animal totem doesn't seem like it could have much to tell you, that could just be your ego talking. The skunk can be a powerful totem to behold, even though it may not seem as glorious as the owl. Nature shows us that every form of life has something to teach us—we just have to listen.

To discover the animal energies that will be your totems, you will need to recognize the animals that you're already drawn to and fascinated by. Use the following questions to help you determine which animals are the most prominent energies in your life.

Have you ever been bitten or attacked by an animal? I've had multiple dreams where I've been bitten on the hand by a snake, specifically between my pointer finger and my thumb. It is believed that if someone survives an attack or was attacked by a specific animal, that this animal is their totem, as the attack was a way of testing their ability to harness that animal's power.

Do you have dreams of animals? This is especially important if the dreams are recurring or continue to take place throughout different periods of your life.

What animals do you see the most when you are outside? Have you encountered any wild animals in your environment? This could include snakes, turtles, or crows, etc.

Do you visit the zoo? What are your feelings about the zoo? Think about which animal you look forward to seeing the most. How does this animal make you feel?

What animal frightens you the most? More often than not, what we fear is what we have to learn to come to terms with. For example, many people are afraid of snakes. When we do this, it becomes an integration of power instead of a fear. The animal that you are most afraid of will help you confront the fears and judgments in order for you to understand the lesson or the medicine that they carry. Some people refer to this energy as your shadow animal, suggesting that this animal will help you with the seemingly darker aspects of yourself that you may want to hide.

Of all the animals in existence, whether alive or dead, what is the one that you have become most fascinated with? If you're drawn to a particular animal and find yourself researching it, looking for pictures of it, finding clothing or decorations featuring it, or you otherwise just want representations of it around you, that could be spiritually significant. You may feel called to learn more about the messages around this animal and the symbolism they contained in society such as the unicorn or the phoenix. Usually the animal that has the most prominent presence for you in your mind is the animal that has a specific message to teach you.

Spirit guides, spirit animals, power animals . . . these are all names for animal totems. No matter what you choose to call them, there are certain aspects that are generally accepted to be true regarding animal medicine. Animal medicine does not cater to religious boundaries or cultural stereotypes. Anyone can learn the deeper meanings of the animal kingdom and apply those lessons to their life.

- Spirit animals that stay with you for your life are usually wild, not domesticated, animals.

- Every animal has its own spirit.

- The animal chooses the person, not the other way around.

- You must develop a relationship with your animal.

- Every animal has its own talents that need to be understood before their specific medicine will be revealed.

- You must honor your animal for its medicine to be effective in your life.

- More than one person can have the same animal spirit.

- Once you learn to connect with the power of your animal, it becomes a doorway to connecting with others. You are never limited to just one totem.

The exercise below will help you meet your spirit animal. It is important to not have any expectation or any judgment when coming into this specific meditation. Let the animal present itself to you, let it choose you—do not force a choice.

Keep in mind that every animal has a specific symbolic meaning to it. The more you learn about this symbology and meditate on it, the more your connection will blossom. Also, don't just accept the first totem that comes up. The imagination in a meditative state is an incredible tool, but if you do not have discernment you can be misled. Before you adhere to a certain spirit animal, ask yourself these six questions:

- What does it make you think of?
- How does it feel?
- Is it an animal that you've been interested in before?
- What sensations does it bring up in you?
- What emotions do you feel?
- What does your heart say?

Think carefully about what you discover before you sit down and begin the following meditation. It is up to you to honestly find your way to the animal totem that will speak most directly to you. Remember that the connection with your animal totem is a deep and profound experience. Be patient with yourself and trust the process. Your animal totem will reveal itself to you in its own time, carrying with it valuable insights and wisdom that will resonate with your inner being. Embrace this sacred journey, and, through the meditation, allow yourself to forge a powerful bond with your animal totem. As you integrate the teachings and symbolism of this special animal into your life, you will find new avenues to explore your metaphysical mindset and deepen your connection to the natural world.

ANIMAL SPIRIT MEDITATION

This meditation will help you reveal what animals are looking to communicate with you. First, relax in a comfortable position, whether that is sitting or lying down. Then, visualize taking ten steps either into a cave or into the trunk of a tree. You will discover that there is a staircase in the space you have entered. This staircase can go up, down, or around—it is up to you.

Take ten steps onto the staircase, counting down from ten to one. As you reach the bottom or the top step, depending upon what direction you are going, you will leave the space and enter into a natural area of your choice. That could be a cliff, a beach, a mountain, the desert . . . whatever resonates with you. Immerse yourself in this experience of nature. Go through each of your senses to form a complete picture of the natural element you are in.

What does it sound like?

What does it look like?

What does it smell like?

What does it taste like on your lips?

What do you feel?

Allow the animal to show up in this natural scene. Pay close attention to its sounds, the color, its movements, and whether it acknowledges your presence. Give thanks for the spirit's making itself known, and ask for it to provide you with confirmation within the next week in this animal form.

Different confirmations can come in different ways. If you see a cheetah in your vision, that doesn't mean a cheetah is going to show up at your L.A. home—but you could find yourself watching a television show where it might appear, or where its characteristics feature prominently. You may encounter figurines, or you might see the animal in a dream. Anything is possible. In any case, you will receive some sign of confirmation once you ask for it.

Bring yourself back to the stairwell and start taking steps, counting from one to ten. Once you arrive at ten, take four deep breaths and allow yourself to feel grounded and connected before you step back into your body. Begin your research process and study the qualities of the animal that was shown to you.

Animal Colors

Here are some other ways to investigate your connection to a particular spirit guide or animal totem.

The color you associate with your animal totem can also help you understand its significance. Each color has both positive and negative qualities. Here are just a few:

Color	Negative Attributes	Positive Attributes
Black	Sacrifice or Secrecy	Birth and Protection
Yellow or Gold	Disparagement	Optimism and Inspiration
Orange	Pride	Creativity and Joy
Green	Uncertain Greed	Healing Growth
Blue	Depression	Calm Happiness
Violet	Obsession	Humility
Gray	Imbalance	Imagination
White	Depletion	Purity
Red	Aggression	Passion

Animal Directions

Paying attention to where and when you see an animal will also give you some deeper insight into what they are trying to tell you. Below is a list of the characteristics and energies of the cardinal directions. If you see a bird while you are driving, note what direction the bird is flying. Pay attention to where the animal is in relation to yourself: is it to the right or left? How does it move: toward you or away from you?

North: Alchemy, empathic intuition, sacred wisdom, teaching, thankfulness, and balance.

East: New beginnings, communication, illumination, intuition, strength of will, and healing.

South: Trust, change, protection, playfulness, overcoming obstacles, and faith.

West: Dreams, emotions, creative arts, higher compassion, and journeys.

In 2018, one of my clients held a women's retreat nestled in the majestic Rocky Mountains, a group of women gathered to embark on a transformative journey. Surrounded by the breathtaking beauty of the Rockies, they sought to connect with their inner selves and find spiritual guidance through the exploration of animal totems in the wild.

As the weekend went by, the women participated in various activities, from guided meditations to silent walks in the wilderness. Each woman approached the experience with an open heart and a yearning to connect with the natural world on a deeper level.

On the final day of the retreat, as they prepared to bid farewell to this sacred space, a sense of gratitude and unity filled the air. During the closing ceremony, one by one the women shared their reflections on the transformative journey they had just undertaken.

To the astonishment of all, a recurring theme emerged—each woman had encountered a wolf during their time in the mountains. Some had seen wolves in dreams, while others had spotted them from afar during their silent walks.

The wolf, known for its strength, resilience, and deep sense of intuition, had become a powerful symbol of unity, courage, and guidance for these women. They realized that the wolf was a reflection of their collective journey, representing the strength they found within themselves and the unyielding connection they had forged with one another.

The story of the wolf's crossing their paths became a cherished tale among the women, a reminder of the profound bond they shared and the transformative power of nature in guiding their souls.

CHAPTER 13

CRYSTAL BEINGS

As humans, we have a consciousness that we are aware of, and we know that other species that inhabit the planet also have this or a similar form of consciousness. We are aware that plants can react to stimuli like light and touch, and may even have the ability to make decisions and "learn" from what they have experienced. In the same way, animals are self-aware: species as diverse as cats, chimpanzees, and dolphins have the capacity to recognize themselves in a mirror. And while minerals seem less likely to be able to be aware in that way, it has been theorized that the crystals of the Earth also hold a consciousness.

Are Crystals Conscious?

A researcher named Alexander Berezin, PhD, has proposed plausible quantum models for the action of healing crystals. The concept underlying his finding is called "isotopicity."

Isotopes are atoms of the same element (which, in other words, contain a unique number of protons and electrons) with different properties due to varying numbers of neutrons. Crystals form isotopic neural networks because of the different isotopes they contain, similar to how neurons in our brain communicate. This is not magic; it's a chemical phenomenon. For example, quartz, a popular healing crystal, has different isotopes of oxygen and silicon, making it potentially more diverse and intelligent than we are.

Crystals and Memory

The concept of living in a crystal matrix is rooted in the belief that crystals play a fundamental role in the structure and functioning of the universe. According to this idea, crystals form the underlying framework or matrix that influences and supports all living beings and the environment.

Proponents of this belief suggest that crystals possess unique energetic properties that interact with various aspects of life, including human consciousness and the Earth's energy field. This crystal matrix is said to create a network of interconnected energy patterns that influence the flow of energy and information throughout the universe.

In this context, the crystal matrix is considered to be a dynamic and intelligent system, constantly exchanging information and energy with living beings. The presence of crystals in our surroundings is believed to have an impact on our well-being, emotional state, and even spiritual growth.

Water is one of the five primary elements that comprise the world, along with fire, earth, air, and the Akash (the spirit, or ether). Because water is a soft crystalline structure that contains three isotopes of oxygen and two isotopes of hydrogen, it can provide a substantial capacity for the storage and transmission of homeopathic patterns. In Dr. Masaru Emoto's famous study of the effects of emotion on water, he proved that this element reacts to the energetic properties of the consciousnesses surrounding it. Crystalline structures such as ice can hold on to love and pain—and that capacity can be extended to the mineral structures we refer to as crystals. (In the movie *Frozen*, lovable snowman Olaf tells the princess that the water has memory. This kind of aside in popular culture is like an Easter egg given to people who might want to go deeper and find these things out!)

Ancient Crystals

Crystals have been seen as a source of power and higher knowledge for thousands of years. To benefit from crystals and open oneself up to a metaphysical mindset, you can engage in practices that go beyond the traditional approach to crystal healing. Here are some ways to tap into the deeper metaphysical aspects of working with crystals:

By approaching crystals with an open mind and heart, we can unlock their potential for spiritual transformation, higher consciousness, and a profound metaphysical connection to the universe and their inner selves. Remember, the key is to be receptive to the energies of these ancient crystals and allow them to guide us on our journey of self-discovery and enlightenment.

As we spoke of earlier, the stronger your energy field is, the more you project that field out. Because a crystal oscillates at its own frequency, it is constantly creating a larger vibrational field affecting the nervous system and transmitting information to the brain.

So, the next time you feel called to a certain crystal, it might be because your electromagnetic field and the crystals like pneumatic field are in sync, and that this could actually be a good crystal that would work with you and bring more into your life.

Meditation and Contemplation: Incorporate crystals into your meditation practice to enhance your connection with their energies. Hold a crystal in your hand, place it on your body, or simply focus your gaze on its patterns and colors during meditation.

Crystal Grids for Intentions: Create crystal grids with crystals to amplify intentions and manifestations. Arrange crystals in sacred geometric patterns and infuse them with your goals and desires. The combination of specific crystals and sacred geometry can amplify and align your intentions with the universe's energy.

Ancestral Connections: Explore the historical significance of ancient crystals and their use in ancient civilizations. Connect with the wisdom of your ancestors and explore how they utilized crystals for spiritual growth and healing. This can provide a deeper understanding of your roots and heritage, fostering a profound sense of connection and guidance.

Rituals and Ceremonies: Incorporate ancient crystal rituals and ceremonies into your spiritual practices. Honor the wisdom of the past by engaging in sacred rituals that involve ancient crystals, fostering a sense of reverence and respect for the energies they hold.

Astral Travel and Akashic Records: Use ancient crystals as tools to facilitate astral travel and access the Akashic records. These crystals are believed to possess the ability to attune one's consciousness to higher realms and unlock hidden knowledge about the universe and oneself.

Intuitive Crystal Work: Embrace your intuition and allow it to guide you in selecting and working with ancient crystals. Instead of following traditional guidelines, trust your instincts to choose crystals that resonate with your soul and support your metaphysical journey.

Elemental Connections: Explore the elemental energies of ancient crystals and their connection to nature. Engage in grounding practices by spending time in nature with these crystals, fostering a deeper appreciation for the interconnectedness of all living beings.

CHAPTER 14

MYCELIUM: THE EARTH'S NEURAL NETWORK

Under your feet is an entire network of interconnected cells that are both feeding and, later, decomposing living (or formerly living) organisms. This is the neural network of the planet. Mycelium is a tubular thread of cells that spreads through the soil and connects the roots of plants to each other. This network communicates with each other and shares information, feeding off the waste on the planet. In the metaphysical mindset, we can draw parallels between the interconnected neural network of our planet and the inner workings of our consciousness. Just as our minds are filled with thoughts and emotions that connect and influence each other, so too does the mycelium link the roots of plants and share vital information.

The mycelium serves as a reminder that we are all part of a greater web of existence, where energy and knowledge flow freely between living organisms. Like the mycelial network, our thoughts and intentions ripple through the collective consciousness, affecting not only ourselves but also the world around us. By tapping into this interconnectedness, we can gain a deeper understanding of our place in the universe and the impact we have on it.

Just as the mycelium feeds off the waste on the planet, we too can learn to transmute negativity and challenges into opportunities for growth and transformation. By aligning ourselves with the natural cycles of life and learning to communicate with the energies of the Earth, we can harness the power of the mycelial network to support our metaphysical journey.

As we explore the neural network of the planet and its remarkable ability to adapt and thrive, we can reflect on the resilience and interconnectedness of all living beings. This understanding can inspire us to cultivate a metaphysical mindset that embraces unity, compassion, and a deep sense of connection with the world around us.

Mycelium is the vegetative part of a fungus, consisting of a vast network of thread-like structures called hyphae. It plays a crucial role in the decomposition of organic matter and the recycling of nutrients in ecosystems. However, mycelium is not limited to its ecological functions. Certain species of fungi, such as *Psilocybe cubensis*, commonly known as "magic mushrooms," contain a compound called psilocybin.

Psilocybin is a naturally occurring psychedelic compound that belongs to the tryptamine family. When ingested, psilocybin is converted into psilocin, which acts as a serotonin receptor agonist in the brain. This interaction leads to alterations in perception, cognition, and consciousness, resulting in the characteristic psychedelic experience. Research suggests that psilocybin-assisted therapy may be effective in treating conditions such as depression, anxiety, PTSD, and addiction.

The psychedelic experience induced by psilocybin is often described as profound and transformative. It can provide individuals with new insights, increased self-awareness, and a sense of connection to the world around them. These experiences can have a lasting impact on your beliefs.

As the field of psychedelic research continues to evolve, there is growing recognition of the therapeutic potential of substances like psilocybin. However, it is important to note that the use of psychedelics should always be approached with caution, in a controlled and supportive environment, under the guidance of trained professionals.

Connecting with the Mycelial Network

For this meditation, you don't need to work with psilocybin. It's possible to benefit from the mushroom kingdom without directly working with it—after all, it physically surrounds us at all times. I will talk more in the next chapter about how to connect with a plant's spirit. Find a serene place where you can sit comfortably and undisturbed. Take a few deep breaths to relax your mind and body.

1. **Grounding Meditation:** Begin by visualizing roots extending from the soles of your feet, burrowing deep into the Earth. Imagine these roots reaching the mycelial network below, interweaving with the intricate threads of the mycelium. Feel yourself becoming one with the Earth's neural network.

2. **Open Awareness:** With your mind's eye, picture the mycelial network spreading beneath the soil, connecting various plants and organisms. Allow yourself to feel the flow of information and energy pulsing through this vast interconnected web.

3. **Intention-Setting:** Set your intention to tap into the collective wisdom and insights held within the mycelial network. State a question or seek guidance from the interconnected intelligence of the Earth.

4. **Silent Listening:** Sit in silent contemplation, opening yourself to receive any messages, sensations, or images that come to you. Embrace your role as a conscious participant in this profound communication with nature.

5. **Gratitude and Connection:** Express your gratitude to the mycelial network for its guidance and interconnectedness. Feel the sense of oneness and unity with all living beings on the planet.

6. **Journal Reflection:** After the meditation, take a few moments to jot down any insights, experiences, or feelings that arose during the practice. Reflect on how this connection with the mycelial network deepens your metaphysical mindset and enhances your connection with nature.

Repeat this exercise whenever you feel the need to reconnect with the natural world's wisdom, and experience the profound unity that lies within the mycelial network. As you continue this practice, you may find yourself developing a deeper appreciation for the Earth's interconnectedness and gaining valuable insights on your spiritual journey. Maybe you'll start to see a grid along the globe.

PSILOCYBIN MEDITATION

Here is a guided meditation to do when working with psilocybin.

1. Find a calm and comfortable space where you can relax without any distractions. Close your eyes and take a few deep breaths, allowing yourself to settle into the present moment.

2. Visualize yourself surrounded by a warm, soothing light. Feel this light enveloping your entire body, bringing a sense of relaxation and peace.

3. Set an intention for your journey with psilocybin. What do you hope to gain or explore? Focus on this intention and hold it in your mind as you continue with the meditation.

4. As the psilocybin begins to take effect, pay attention to any sensations or emotions that arise within your body. Allow yourself to fully experience them without judgment or resistance. Chant the mantra "No Judgment, No Expectation" when needing a reminder.

5. Imagine yourself walking through a beautiful forest, with sunlight streaming through the canopy of trees. Feel the earth beneath your feet and the gentle breeze on your skin. Take note of where you are. Is it familiar? Is anyone there with you?

6. As you continue walking, notice any thoughts or beliefs that may be holding you back or causing you distress. Acknowledge them, and then imagine them floating away like leaves on a stream, leaving you feeling lighter and more at peace.

7. Take a moment to connect with your guides and intuition. Ask yourself any questions you may have or seek guidance on a specific issue. Trust that the answers will come to you in their own time.

8. Spend some time simply being present in nature, observing the beauty and serenity around you. Allow yourself to feel a deep sense of gratitude for this experience and for the healing potential of psilocybin.

9. When you feel ready, slowly bring your awareness back to the present moment. Take a few deep breaths and open your eyes, feeling refreshed and renewed.

It's important to approach these experiences with caution and respect for the powerful nature of psychedelics. Now, let's go into the fascinating world of psychedelics and explore their potential for healing and personal growth.

CHAPTER 15

PLANT-SPIRIT MEDICINE

Working with the spirit of a plant should be approached as an intentional practice. Similar to how someone would spend time in their garden talking to their plants, it's a symbiotic relationship when you shift your energy to recognize that the plant also has a "consciousness" or awareness.

I learned more about how plants can react to our energetic field, or even be affected by our intentions, by studying the electromagnetic frequencies they give off. I learned about this through working with a device that recognizes the electromagnetic signals that a plant has with a device similar to an EKG machine. The machine fits in the palm of your hand and essentially is a MIDI controller with nodes that attach to it. You place the nodes (similar to what you'd be hooked up to in the hospital) on the plant's leaves and flowers. Then the device will recognize the electromagnetic frequency of the plant and will translate it into sound using the musical scale. The sound that comes from the device can be played as a piano, strings, or chimes; but what is most interesting is how unhealthy plants seem to play a discordant tune, while the healthy plants play more melodic sounds. This interaction allowed me to experiment for a few months with giving Reiki to plants and measuring the output of the music they made. I found that the more attention I gave a plant, the "happier" the music coming from it appeared to be. I listened to the plants in my backyard, at commercial cannabis operations, and when I would go camping in the mountains. The common theme that I found was that when you intentionally interact with the plants, they will have changes in their electromagnetic output, and this can be audibly heard. One particular instance was during an event I participated in which was dubbed in *Rolling Stone* as "The Best Pot Party." During this event, guests would come into different rooms and have an immersive experience centered around the cannabis plant. In one room, you were blindfolded and ate cannabis-infused food; in another room you were guided into a sound-healing meditation with the music of a cannabis plant. During this event, I was leading the sound-healing portion of the meditation and attaching the device to a small cannabis plant for the attendees to listen to the music of the plant. One distinct moment was when I told the guests to notice the melody of the plant as we started the meditation, and then I told them to pay attention to any changes and raise their hand if they heard any. As I said this, I started giving the plant Reiki, and the melody, pitch, and tone all changed. Everyone raised their hands and was aware of the plant's change in frequency. This was the first public display I had done with Reiki, cannabis, and the concept of the spirit of the plant's responding to human contact. During this event, I also placed the nodes on each of my hands and showed the group how the device could also measure the vibrations of humans.

Each guest walked out of the event that night with a new understanding of how they interact with different plant medicines and how the power of their intention can have a measurable effect on the plants and people around them. Was it the plant's spirit connecting through the device? We may never truly know, but the entire experience allowed the guests to comprehend that the plants communicate and can fluctuate based on intentional interactions such as giving the plant Reiki or physical touch.

When approaching any type of plant, whether it's to admire or work with the plant on a spiritual level, this story reminds me to come to any plant with grace and appreciation. Pay attention to what plants you are drawn to work with and those that elicit strong feelings or memories. Intentionally working with a plant spirit involves forming a conscious and respectful connection with the energetic essence or consciousness of a particular plant. Just like working with animal spirits, it is a practice of building a relationship with the spirit of the plant and learning from its wisdom and healing properties. Here are some steps and guidance to approach working with a plant spirit:

1. **Research and Choose a Plant:** Start by researching different plants and their spiritual and healing properties. Choose a plant that resonates with you, or one that you feel drawn to. It could be a plant you encounter frequently in your surroundings, or one that holds specific significance to your spiritual journey.

2. **Create Sacred Space:** Find a quiet and peaceful space where you can connect with the plant spirit without distractions. Create a sacred space through meditation, lighting candles, or using incense to set the intention for your practice.

3. **Mindful Observation:** Spend time with the plant in its natural environment. Observe its growth patterns, colors, texture, and any unique features. Pay attention to how it interacts with other beings around it, such as insects or mammals.

4. **Meditative Connection:** Sit or stand near the plant and enter into a meditative state. Take deep breaths and allow your mind to quieten. Focus your attention on the plant and invite its spirit to connect with yours.

5. **Respectful Communication:** Approach the plant spirit with respect and humility. Ask for permission to work with its energy and be open to receiving its guidance. You can communicate through thoughts, intentions, or spoken words.

6. **Receive and Interpret Messages:** Be receptive to any insights, sensations, or emotions that arise during your connection with the plant spirit. Trust your intuition and

interpret the messages you receive in a way that feels meaningful to you.

7. **Gratitude and Offerings:** Show your gratitude to the plant spirit for its presence and teachings. Consider offering something back to the plant as a token of appreciation, such as a small gift, water, or a simple prayer.

8. **Continuing Relationship:** Keep nurturing your connection with the plant spirit through regular visits or meditations. Notice how the relationship evolves over time and how the plant's energy influences your life.

Working with a plant spirit is a deeply personal and intuitive practice. Just like with animal spirits, it requires an open heart, mindfulness, and a willingness to listen and learn. Through intentional connection with plant spirits, you can gain insights into their healing properties and use them for spiritual growth.

Let me share a story of manifestation with you. In the same year I started intentionally working with a certain plant spirit, I manifested finding the love of my life—and as of this writing, you will be happy to know that we are married and finally live together after seven long years. But let me start at the beginning.

The year was 2017, and I was living in Denver, Colorado. While I lived in Colorado, I spent much of my time advocating for—and educating people about working with—plant spirits such as cannabis. I started a series of workshops called the Green Lodge Goddess Gathering. The Green Lodge promoted empowerment, support, and help in establishing vibrational daily practices aimed at personal growth. Each lodge contained educational information about cannabis, frequency, energy healing, Reiki, animal medicine, shamanic and indigenous tools, and esoteric knowledge. Each month, we would gather with an array of healers who ranged from small businesswomen to yogis, meditation experts, shamanic drummers, Reiki Masters, aromatherapists, dance and fitness instructors, Akashic record readers, and more. I hoped to take a little of what had helped me heal in difficult times and combine it with wisdom from these healers to create a whole new experience: honoring tradition while creating something new for ourselves.

Getting to know one another was healing in and of itself. I loved talking to the people who identified as women who came to take part in the communal passing of the peace pipe. I have to say, smoking indoors in a public space is cool. It's even cooler to do this with a bunch of others who are coming together to use cannabis in a thoughtful way. It's not just about getting stoned: it's about connecting through the use of cannabis to relax everyone and make them more comfortable in the environment. It's amazing what a little safe space and some like-minded women can do for your soul. I felt like anything I were to do or say would be accepted, and that feeling takes you places.

After completing five of the Lodges in Denver from the months of January to May, I brought this workshop to California. I've always wanted to live in California, ever since I learned that my mother lived there. As I got to the Airbnb where I was staying, I started talking to the owners. One of them was a woman who was a shadow worker. She said a few things to me that no one else would have known, and I told her why I was in Los Angeles: that I was coming here to do work and hold space with the plant spirit of cannabis in order to educate and inspire people I could reach. She then gave me a plant spirit that she knew I had not worked with but believed would be a delightful companion for me. She looked me dead in the eyes and told me not to use it until I was ready.

Something changed in the year that I started doing these workshops: I now understand that I had been denying filling my cup and continually enmeshed myself in other people's frequencies, and it was only hurting me. I had two wonderful children and what appeared to be eleven relationships, but in reality I was going through the day-to-day fully being a mother and not being anything else. Six months after I received this plant spirit, I decided that I would take a quick trip back to California to see a concert for my birthday. That concert ended up being the Roots.

The day that I arrived in San Francisco for the concert, I immediately looked up the directions to a metaphysical store. The store was called the Sword and Rose. I had never been there, and I had known no one who had recommended this store. I looked on Google and saw the amazing photos of what appeared to be many potions and oils on the wall, and then I knew exactly where I wanted to go. I showed up to this place and immediately wondered if my directions were off, because it looked like any one of the Victorian homes you see in the Bay, specifically in the Haight-Ashbury area. I got out of the car and wandered around what appeared to be a giant house with multiple shops in it, none of which was the store I was looking for. I walked into a candle shop, looking very confused and almost ready to give up. Right away, the woman at the register asked "Are you looking for the Sword and Rose?" And I said yes and how did you know? She replied "We get you guys all the time—go back out the door and immediately to your right, then walk down the alleyway."

I left the store and looked around, trying to figure out what alleyway she was talking about. Suddenly, I realized I was standing right next to something out of Harry Potter: a brick doorway that you cannot see unless you are right next to it, which reveals an alleyway. I walked through the alleyway, past a garden and some statues of Greek gods, then into a little corner space probably no bigger than 400 square feet. As I walked in, the first thing I saw was a man selling his cannabis plants that he harvested with malachite and crystal quartz, which were molded onto the slender stalks of plants to make them look like giant wizard staffs. Immediately, I knew I was in the right place.

I walked up to the counter and told the woman behind the register that I didn't really know why I was here. I said, "All I know is that something is going to happen this weekend and I really need to be grounded. This is my second time in California, and I feel really guided by my mother, who used to paint angels all the time."

The woman behind the counter said a few things to me and brought a smile to my face, and we exchanged a good laugh. She then turned around to the wall of potions and oils, which had drawn me into the store in the first place, and pulled down a bottle of blended oil called "Archangel."

I instantly saw that this was another calling card from my mom. The woman handed me the oil and told me how to use it.

She told me to use it during meditation at the start of my day, by dabbing a small dot on my left wrist, touching that to my right wrist and then my right wrist to my left wrist, then touching my third eye. I took in everything she said before leaving. I got in my car and drove up to the town that I would be staying in, Sebastopol. The next day was the concert. I woke up in the morning and started my seventeenth day of meditation practice. I went outside to do my meditation with this new oil, and everything just felt different. I realized that I felt a knowing and clarity like I hadn't before.

I had the best day, full of love and laughter. By the time the day began to end and the concert was about to begin, I felt like I didn't need anything more: I had already had a perfect experience. I was standing with a friend, relaxed and enjoying myself, when I saw someone walk by. He was wearing a black leather jacket, blue jeans, and a white shirt, with a red hat. I was wearing red lipstick, a black leather jacket, blue jeans, and a white shirt. It looked like we had dressed as a couple in matching outfits with corresponding items. This was the moment . . . I felt I had been preparing for it, somehow. Would I let him walk away and not say anything, or would I follow my gut and go after him? I got up and followed him out of the booth so I could talk to him. Little did I know that this was the beginning of finding the love of my life. Within five minutes we were in deep conversation, laughing and talking—and throughout the whole experience, I felt something so familiar.

We learned that we both worked specifically with the plant cannabis in different ways, and found that we both felt like we'd known each other a long time. After dancing they played "You Got Me," and I realized—something is different about this person. He asked me if there was someone who tells me I'm beautiful every day, and sadly I had to say no, because although I was living in the same home with someone and taking care of my kids and raising my children with them, I was not in a loving, fulfilling relationship. That's very hard to admit out loud, and it's even harder to realize that you're living a lie in order to keep somebody else happy. I was going through the motions, not being intimate with my partner, living like roommates. I didn't want my children to grow up and see that as a representation of what they thought a mom and a dad looked like or were. I want my children to see an expressive, blissful, exuberant love, and I don't want them to settle because they think they are tied down. Working with plant spirit helps you realize that if you feel a discord within a relationship or a friendship, you're most likely not alone in that feeling.

As it happened, this man was staying in the same house as me—a giant Airbnb coordinated by a friend of mine. We all went back to the house that night after having dinner, and in the car on the way back we were listening to the Chill station on Sirius XM, which typically plays House music but this night played "Higher Love" by Steve Winwood. As this man, who had been a stranger yesterday, sat in the car with me, driving back on that road in Northern California, we suddenly knew—we had been brought together by something that was bigger than ourselves. We

Joe's Experience

I spoke to my dear friend Joe Moore, founder of the podcast *Psychedelics Today*, about his experiences. Here are a few words from Joe about his experience with psychedelics, and his insights on the process of integration, meaning the process of assimilating and incorporating the insights, emotions, and changes that occur during that experience into your daily life and understanding of self. It is a period of time when you are acutely aware of how the experience has impacted you and how it influences your thoughts, feelings, and actions.

"The first big session I did with Ayahuasca, I was pretty young. And it was a little scary. I had done a bunch of holistic breathwork before, and I was used to a level of integration post-experience, given my breathwork community. And there is near zero integration work as part of this experience—they actually allowed people to drive home that day.

"I hear the word 'integration' about eighty times per week, and my response is 'Great, tell me what you think that is, because I probably disagree.' How I want to set people up for integration is, hopefully, that they have a lot of free time to dedicate to this entire process. And a lot of them might not have that kind of free time, so they should carefully consider: can you afford to be destabilized right now? They should really carefully consider that when deciding to go in. They should also figure out practices for self-pampering, they should dedicate time for artistic expression and journaling, long walks in nature if possible—like, a really gentle self-pampering self-exploratory thing for a good two weeks after. Try to lay down some good habits like waking up and drinking water and doing yoga, or something like that.

"You don't need somebody to help you with your integration, though that can be helpful: there are tools out there. *Psychedelics Today* has actually put out a couple workbooks, a trip journal and an integration workbook that can really help people through the difficulty of the process.

"We are entering this fantastic world and are having experiences that have very little to do with our weird Western-world civilization. You will probably have a realization that a lot of the world is pretty sick. So then what do you do? Do you immediately quit everything and go live in the ashram or whatever it is for you? To me, the answer was to go slow and follow your gut: explore things. Conduct cheap experiments versus expensive experiments. An expensive experiment would be to sell everything you own and give all the money to a charity, then move to an ashram a week or two after your experience. You might regret that. The more careful thing to do is to enter into this new frame of mind more slowly and deliberately. Maybe it's trying jiu-jitsu. Maybe it's running a marathon. Maybe it's spending more time in nature. Maybe it's building a giant crab car for Burning Man." (Joe's wife actually did this!) "Whatever it may be for that person: it is about the experience. Find the things that make your soul sing."

felt like we had tapped into the quantum, and we got so clear about what we wanted that there was no choice but for it to happen.

I moved to Colorado, and that's where my soul sang about creating this space and educating others about what I had learned and how I would use it to help other people. That developed into the workshops, which later developed into the *Metaphysical Cannabis Oracle Deck*, and now has evolved into this book. Throughout the past decade, I have worked with different plant spirits, and I highly recommend approaching working with plants as if they embody a consciousness similar to someone who is your friend or someone who has your best interest at heart. You'll be so surprised at what can happen when you open yourself up to the quantum potential that exists when you decide to have an awareness of yourself and the nature and environment around you.

There are so many things in this world that are here to work with us to provide us a better quality of life, to provide us with a more improved human experience. I hope this story inspires you to work with plant consciousness more and more. Even the plants that are in your house, or the plants that are in your garden. Express an interest in working with them as authentically as you can. And watch what happens in your life whenever you live authentically and ask for help from the other companions that share and inhabit this world with you.

CHAPTER 16

PSYCHEDELIC PLANT SPIRITS

How do you know working with a psychedelic plant spirit will not lead you down a deep dark hole into the worst trip of your entire life, because you haven't solved some of your trauma, but you still want to work with the plant spirit? The answer is that you don't.

There's no guarantee that your interaction with plant psychedelics is going to be a wonderful experience. But when you engage with plant medicine, and psychedelic plant medicine specifically, and you come in with the intention to have no judgment or expectations, you are setting yourself up to connect more consciously with the quantum field and making its vast dimensions available to you. You will have to keep your mind clear to decipher and integrate the messages that you are going to receive, and that is the most important part of the experience. This information is often called "downloads." You can get downloads at any point in time, just like a revelation. When you are working with psychedelic plant spirits specifically and intentionally, these downloads can come in many shapes and forms, so it is vital to have discernment when trying to untangle these messages.

When we discussed Reiki, we went through the process of developing an awareness of your body and how it shows you what you need to know. The same kind of channeling based on the senses will lead you to figure out what the plant spirit is trying to tell you. You may hear the message, you may feel it, or you might see it through the three central parts of your body: the head, the heart, and the gut. If you feel something in any of these areas when you start to receive a message, pay close attention and write it down. Keep repeating to yourself that there is no expectation and no judgment. Just like we talked about going into the Akashic records with a query, it's vital to have a question, an understanding, or an intention in mind when you are deciding to work with a psychedelic plant spirit.

In order to get the most relevant information for your current circumstance, it is important to set an intention; otherwise, you can be inundated with information and harsh messages that you won't be able to perceive well. Because the brain only knows how to communicate in symbols that it's already seen, don't take these messages at face value. Once you're able to decipher the message about what your brain is showing you, things that seem odd or out of sorts become clearer.

At this point in the book, you understand energetically how the body works, which can help you take care of yourself as you receive messages. There are many traditions that harp on the importance of purification and preparation before entering a space with a psychedelic plant. There are many calls for no sex, no meat, no sugar because these are considered aspects of our human experience that cloud our channel. It's quite odd that there is an influx of products pairing sugar with psychedelic plant spirits in order to mass-market and capitalize on the use of psychedelic plants. Sugar triggers the body's response to dopamine, so it's almost like a placebo if you are trying to use a plant spirit but it's coated in processed food and sweeteners. When an individual eats sugar, the brain produces huge amounts of dopamine. This is like how the brain responds when it has substances like cocaine or heroin. Therefore, I believe it is vital to source plant spirits that are not combined with sugar.

It's important to remember that plants have world spirits. That means they exist on the physical plane and they have needs: although they differ slightly from humans, our needs are the same. They still need food and water and to be grown and loved. Plants have played tricks on those who do not have respect or appreciation for their medicine. There have been many stories of people traveling to Peru to take Ayahuasca, only to be spoken to during their experience by entities that they perceived to be not very nice. Sometimes these entities have told them to do disturbing things to themselves. When these people came out of the session with the plant spirit, they felt even worse than when they went in.

Your truth may not be everybody else's truth, and this is a very important aspect to keep in mind when you are working with the plant spirit. And although you may believe that your truth is that you have been sent here to save the world or to fulfill some giant mission, be wary of messages from plants that stroke your ego. Remember what we learned earlier about the unified field: we are all the chosen ones. There are so many people that claim to be informed by the plant spirits, guides of the plant spirits, descendants of Nibiru, descendants of Atlantis, indigo children, crystal children—every egoic title that you can think of has been claimed. Each plant carries a different message for a different person, and it's believed by some that each person has a golden blueprint for a certain plant that will heal all their ailments, because it aligns with their genetic makeup. Here are some common messages that have been shared by those who use different psychedelic plant spirits.

Ayahuasca

Many people come to sit with Mother Ayahuasca when they face some sort of crisis. Many people who I have known sat with Ayahuasca because they had some kind of terminal or life-threatening illness. One woman I spoke to described being dragged down to what felt like a deep, dark, wet tree trunk surrounded by a pit of snakes, and the snake continued to wrap around her womb. This was a symbol that she was there to heal the cancerous tumors that had manifested in her womb. The message that she received from the Ayahuasca was that she was not trusting herself. The description of the vine leading to the underworld in a somewhat empty and dark space is reminiscent of many people's experiences with the plant spirit. Sometimes this plant speaks in metaphors, and sometimes she speaks literally to you. It depends on how you perceive the truth.

Cactus

I do have an affinity for the messages that come from the San Pedro cactus. They are very grounding messages, and I feel like when I worked with the San Pedro cactus my own abilities and awareness increased and enhanced tenfold. The messages from the cactus usually appear very hard-opening, and it is a very grounding and practical medicine that is becoming more popularized in the microdosing community. Messages that you receive from the heart or the gut are extremely trustworthy; when working with this psychedelic plant spirit, it is an easier pathway if you are walking the path of forgiveness.

Mushrooms

I was told I was allergic to cannabis, and I believed my mother. But when I was about eighteen years old, I had a thought that maybe I'm not allergic to mushrooms and psilocybin; so not only did I dive in to working with this plant spirit, but it became my soulmate. Just as there are different cultivars or strains of cannabis, there are many species of mushrooms. Mushrooms for me always bring the message "lighten up." Life is full of fun and those magic moments that seem to just pop up out of nowhere, even when it's rainy and dark outside. Some people find that mushrooms have a trickster energy, but I have not had that experience myself. There have been plenty of times that I have taken edibles made of chocolate infused with mushrooms, and I fell asleep. This is another reason that I don't like when psychedelic plants are used with an inhibitor. For me, the message that always comes through with mushrooms is to not take yourself so seriously, and live a little. And laugh a lot.

Cannabis

The key messages from the cannabis plant spirit that I see being shared the most are those of love, heart-centered consciousness, and focus. I attribute a lot to my relationship with the plant spirit of cannabis and how this plant spirit has helped and enhanced my manifestations, state of mind, mindset, and ability to create in my life. Once I stopped fearing this plant and began regarding it and showing it respect, there were so many aspects of my life that fell into place and provided me with a deeper sense of clarity.

This meditation is a significant starting point for you to work with the plant spirit on a dimensional level. If you are ready to do this meditation and you have chosen the plant spirit you're going to work with, you know how to read your signs; you are ready to create this new reality by firing these new neural pathways and really becoming the one in charge of how you feel, think, and move through this reality: this is the meditation you've been waiting for.

Begin in a comfortable position, either seated or lying down. In this meditation we are going to move through the human dimensions composing the soul, the awareness, the heart, the mind, the energy, and the body. Allow the eyes to close and become aware of the space around your eyes. Allow everything that happened today, or that is going to happen, to slowly fade away like the colors washing out. You are aware of the surrounding space in all directions in every way: east, west, north, and south. You are aware of the space around your body, and you are aware of your body.

Bring your awareness to the top of your head and your face. Do you feel any sensation in any particular area? What are the sensations? Just notice them and sit with them. Maybe it is tightness, maybe it is a piercing between your eyes, maybe it is heat. Whatever it is, feel into the sensation and feel that it is neutral. Bring a nonjudgmental awareness to the sensation that you feel, and let it rise and fall away. Shift your attention down to your throat and your neck. What does it feel like here? Is it warm? Is it hot? Allow that nonjudgmental awareness of the sensation to come, and let the sensation pass. Now bring your awareness to your shoulders, your arms, and down to your elbows. Continue to your forearms, your wrists, your hands, and the fingers. Bring your awareness to your chest and your heart. Place your hand on your heart and notice the beat. Notice the space around your heart. Does it feel closed, tight, or somewhere in between? Stay in that nonjudgmental awareness and move your attention down to your stomach. Place all your attention and awareness of the sensations on your belly and your lower back. Move your attention slowly up to your shoulders and your back, aware of the tension or lack of tension in between your shoulder blades. Notice any tension or lack of tension between your tailbone and your sacrum. Place your awareness on your hips, and take note if you feel any pressure. Allow your awareness to move down your legs, thighs, hamstrings, and knees. Then, let it move down your shins and your calves, all the way down to your feet and toes. Finally, expand this field to the entire body as one quantum form.

Now we are going to move into the energetic dimension. Here is where we will connect this dimension by bringing your awareness to the moment of your breath which is connected to your life force. Notice your breaths as you breathe in and out. How long is each inhalation? How long is each exhalation? Find a balance in your breaths with a mindful breath pattern, such as breathing in for the same count, holding it, and breathing out for the same count. Be aware of the breath moving in through your nose and out through your mouth. Be aware of how far the breath goes down into your belly and if you feel this breath in your chest. If you feel this in your nose, become aware of that as well. Hold your focus with your breath, wherever it is. Now we are going to move into the dimension of the mind. Bring awareness to the thoughts that are coming in and out of your brain. See the thoughts that are coming out of the void and allow them to dissipate back into the void. See the void as a big black ocean of the mind that brings ideas in and pulls them back out. Notice whether your waves are calm or stormy. Whatever, your experience is perfectly yours. Allow these thoughts to come and go and notice your ability to be firm and not swept away with the thoughts. You no longer get caught up in the thinking/feeling loop. You feel the vastness of the void and the spaciousness that allows the ideas to come and go with ease.

Now we will go into the fourth dimension of the heart, the home of feeling and emotion. Bring awareness to your heart and ask yourself what you are feeling in this moment. Go deeper into this awareness and see if there is something, such as a deeper emotional connection, that needs to be healed. Simply watch and observe, with no expectation, what shows up for you. Let go and let yourself move through the emotions, and do not try to force anything to happen. Some days when you do this meditation, your emotions may become more intense than others.

Now we are going to move into the fifth dimension of awareness. Imagine that you are stepping into nature. As you step into this natural environment of your choosing, you are going to have a mixture of physical sensations. Watch and observe your breath, your thoughts, and your emotions. Expand the lens of your peripheral, to see beyond and take yourself out of your body as an observer, watching yourself observing. Keep your awareness on this place and allow yourself to see yourself lie down. See yourself relaxed, and then allow yourself to fully relax. You are safe in this space. You cannot be touched. Just let your soul sit in this space and feel the safety.

Now we are coming into the last dimension, the dimension of the soul. This is the space beyond time and form: it is truly unlimited. Sit in the space and let the awareness of stillness find you and sit in that power of stillness. When you are ready, slowly come back to the dimension of awareness and see yourself standing up from the natural environment you brought yourself to. Then from this dimension of awareness, slowly return back to the dimension of your heart. From your heart, slowly follow that presence back to your mind. From your mind, slowly follow that awareness of energy through your body, from your toes up all the way to your head. And lastly, feel yourself stop observing and landing back in your physical body, feeling loved, guided, and supported always. Place your arms above your head toward your back, interlace your fingers, turn your palms down, and stretch out your back and your body from your feet through your toes. Reach a hand forward, draw your thighs into your belly, and then gently roll your way up into a comfortably seated position. Bring your hands to a prayer position in front of your chest and honor yourself, your mindset, your ability to change, and your companion who helped you along the way.

METAPHYSICAL INTENTIONS

Now that you have journeyed with me through the pages of this book, you have learned about programmed mindsets, the laws of physics, and past lives. As you continue your exploration of metaphysical concepts, I encourage you to go deeper into the topics that resonated the most with you, seeking out additional knowledge and insights.

To help you integrate these newfound perspectives into your daily life and foster a deeper understanding of this metaphysical mindset, I offer you a practical tool: a collection of one hundred daily intentions. Use these affirmations as guideposts to start your day, setting the tone for your experiences and interactions.

Each morning, take a moment to read and internalize one of these intentions. Let it become your mantra for the day, keeping it at the fore-front of your mind as you move through your daily tasks and encounters. Whether it's fostering gratitude, embracing self-compassion, or aligning with the energies of the universe, these affirmations can help you bring mindfulness and intentionality to your life.

As you consistently work with these intentions, you will notice a pro-found shift in your thoughts, emotions, and actions. They will serve as anchors for your metaphysical practice, empowering you to embrace a more enlightened and harmonious way of being.

METAPHYSICAL INTENTIONS

I intend to embrace the limitless power of my mind and create the reality I desire.

I intend to release all limiting beliefs and step into my true potential.

I intend to cultivate unwavering self-confidence and trust in my abilities.

I intend to align my thoughts, emotions, and actions with my highest self.

I intend to tap into the infinite abundance of the universe and manifest my desires effortlessly.

I intend to attract positive and empowering relationships into my life.

I intend to let go of fear and embrace a mindset of fearlessness and courage.

I intend to cultivate a deep sense of self-love and acceptance.

I intend to awaken my intuitive abilities and trust my inner guidance.

I intend to connect with my higher self and gain clarity on my life's purpose.

I intend to harness the power of gratitude and to appreciate every aspect of my life.

I intend to cultivate a mindset of resilience and overcome any obstacles that come my way.

I intend to heal and balance my mind, body, and spirit for optimal well-being.

I intend to let go of the need for external validation and find validation within myself.

METAPHYSICAL INTENTIONS

I intend to embrace change and see it as an opportunity for growth and transformation.

I intend to radiate love and compassion to myself and others.

I intend to live in the present moment and find joy in each experience.

I intend to trust the process of life and surrender to the greater intelligence guiding me.

I intend to step up and face imposter syndrome and know that is not my highest self.

I intend to create a harmonious environment that supports my growth and success.

I intend to release events that I could not control and move into a state of alignment.

I intend to tap into the wisdom of the universe and gain profound insights.

I intend to align my thoughts with positive affirmations and reprogram my subconscious mind.

I intend to embrace forgiveness and let go of all resentment and grudges.

I intend to cultivate deep and rich relationships.

I intend to tap into the creative energy within me and express myself authentically.

I intend to break free from societal expectations and live life on my own terms.

METAPHYSICAL INTENTIONS

I intend to nurture my spiritual gifts and dedicate myself to understanding how I will use them.

I intend to let go of comparison and celebrate my unique gifts and talents.

I intend to harness the power of visualization for my daily manifestations.

I intend to release my expectations of situations and move forward with divine bliss.

I intend to let go of scarcity mentality and embrace a mindset of abundance and prosperity.

I intend to cultivate a deep sense of worthiness and deservingness of all good things.

I intend to embrace the lessons presented to me and see them as opportunities for growth.

I intend to live each day with passion, purpose, and enthusiasm.

I intend to surround myself with uplifting and supportive people who believe in me.

I intend to release all resistance and surrender to the flow of life.

I intend to tap into my innate wisdom and make decisions that align with my highest good.

I intend to let go of my desire to tell everyone my side of the story.

I intend to honor and nurture my physical body as a sacred vessel.

I intend to cultivate a deep sense of inner joy that radiates from within.

METAPHYSICAL INTENTIONS

I intend to let go of self-sabotaging behaviors and embrace a mindset of self-empowerment.

I intend to connect with the interconnectedness of all beings and the web of life.

I intend to release all judgments and see the beauty and divinity in all things.

I intend to cultivate a mindset of continuous growth and learning.

I intend to let go of the need for perfection and embrace my authentic self.

I intend to tap into the energy of the universe and allow it to guide and support me.

I intend to release all resistance to change, because it is the only constant.

I intend to embrace vulnerability and live as my most authentic self.

I intend to cultivate a deep sense of gratitude for the smallest things in my life.

I intend to harness the power of positive affirmations and rewire my subconscious mind.

I intend to let go of the past and embrace the infinite possibilities of the present moment.

I intend to connect with my inner child and nurture a sense of playfulness and wonder.

I intend to release all antihero tendencies that limit my potential.

METAPHYSICAL INTENTIONS

I intend to cultivate a deep sense of trust in the unfolding of my life's journey.

I intend to tap into the collective consciousness and to access universal wisdom.

I intend to release all negative attachments and create space for new blessings to enter my life.

I intend to cultivate a mindset of abundance and prosperity in all areas of my life.

I intend to let go of the need for external validation and find validation within myself.

I intend to embrace the power of forgiveness and free myself from the burdens of the past.

I intend to tap into the wellspring of unconditional love within myself and radiate it to others.

I intend to release the need to hold onto obstacles and give grace to those around me.

I intend to cultivate a lifelong respect for myself that exudes out of my being.

I intend to trust my intuition and make decisions that align with my soul's purpose.

I intend to let go of all fears and step into a place of unshakable faith and confidence.

I intend to embrace the interconnectedness of all life and treat every being with love and respect.

METAPHYSICAL INTENTIONS

I intend to release all judgments and accept all outcomes as the highest good for all.

I intend to tap into the well of creativity within me and express my unique gifts to the world.

I intend to let go of self-limiting beliefs and embrace the truth of my unlimited potential.

I intend to nurture my self-care routine before expanding my energy outside of myself.

I intend to release all judgment and criticism and cultivate a mindset of acceptance and compassion.

I intend to harness my ability to visualize a new reality.

I intend to let go of my desire for approval from others and give myself what I am seeking.

I intend to cultivate a deep sense of gratitude for every experience and every lesson in my life.

I intend to embrace change as an opportunity for growth and transformation.

I intend to tap into the unlimited potential that exists around me.

I intend to align everything I do with my most authentic self.

I intend to release the self doubt that was instilled in me as a child.

I intend to create a harmonious and supportive environment that nourishes my mind, body, and spirit.

I intend to let go of my past stories and create a future with my new programming.

METAPHYSICAL INTENTIONS

I intend to tap into my intuition and trust the guidance it provides in every moment.

I intend to align with the natural flow of life and surrender to its greater intelligence.

I intend to release all resistance and allow miracles to unfold in my life.

I intend to let go of my constant need for answers and allow the flow of life to move me.

I intend to cultivate a deep sense of self-love and acceptance, honoring my worthiness of all good things.

I intend to accept my vulnerable parts and embrace myself for who I am.

I intend to connect with the wisdom of my body and listen to its messages and signals.

I intend to release all attachments and find freedom in detachment and non-attachment.

I intend to tap into the power of the present moment and find peace and serenity within it.

I intend to harness the energy of the universe and cocreate my reality with divine assistance.

I intend to let go of the need for external approval and trust in my own inner guidance.

I intend to cultivate a mindset of gratitude and appreciate the blessings that surround me.

I intend to release any attachments I have to other people who do not wish the best for me.

METAPHYSICAL INTENTIONS

I intend to tap into the energy of joy and infuse it into every aspect of my life.

I intend to let go of the need for certainty and embrace the beauty of uncertainty and growth.

I intend to connect with the divine intelligence within me and access its infinite wisdom.

I intend to release all judgments and cultivate a mindset of acceptance and non-judgment.

I intend to tap into the power of my breath and use it as a tool for grounding and centering.

I intend to let go of the past and step fully into the present moment with open-heartedness.

I intend to embrace my uniqueness and celebrate the journey of self-discovery and self-empowerment.

CONCLUSION

Being Metaphysical

The intention behind this book and what I hope you take away from it is that there are practices and experiences that we have every day that go beyond our physical understanding of this planet. It's not enough to make a vision board and say affirmations in the mirror, just hoping that something changes for you. Once you alter the programs that you are running, some of which are not your own, you then start to truly live as your authentic self. We don't know what the beginning of the soul looks like, or how to even find that out; and because each of us is so different, there's not really a clear path to understanding exactly what our soul is here to do. But the fact that we all have these souls that inhabit these bodies that influence the natural and physical world around us is something that should not be taken lightly.

We will have times in our life that are not ideal, when what happens is not what we want to happen. The fact is that we only have control over ourselves and our reactions in those situations. I can't sit here and tell you that each experience that you have will cause some spiritual "aha" moment, or that you'll ever be able to have your life completely figured out—that's not the case at all. The only thing that we can do each day is to create our most authentic self and then radiate that out into everything we encounter. We must try to run programs that remind us that we are infinite, that what we seek is actually inside ourselves, and that we live in this world intertwined with these things, and that they're not all visible.

All the conversations that I have had about this book, and why I wanted this book to become something that expanded on the knowledge in the *Metaphysical Cannabis Oracle Deck,* were essential energetic components to this book's process of coming to life. Every time you become aware of a new program you are beginning to run, or an old program you would like to reconsider, that awareness creates momentum for a change you would like to happen. I would have never published a cannabis tarot deck if I had continued to run the program that my mother instilled in me, intending to protect me by scaring me away from something that eventually provided me with so much guidance and wisdom. Sometimes in our lives we realize that we have been told things by our parents, our friends, our bosses, and the media that don't resonate as truth to us. That little voice saying "that's not true" when you read something or you hear something that doesn't sit right with you? Pay attention to that. And pay attention if you experience that at any point in this book—because that is okay. I'm not telling you that everything in this book is gospel; but what I *am* telling you comes from my experience and the knowledge I have gained from studying these aspects of our physical world. Everything that I have studied in my life has told me that the thoughts you think become the reality you experience.

In the words of Joe Moore, find the things that make your soul sing— and when you find those things, hold on to them. You cannot change unless you change your mindset. The change has to start within, and that begins with being truthful with yourself, being honest about your experiences with other people, and having an understanding that each person has a higher self that's not on display in their physical body. Sometimes we get glimpses of that and sometimes we meet people who are full-on embodying living their etheric soulful selves.

It's not enough to know that you are a soul—now you have to figure out what your soul is trying to say to you. It's time to dive into those deeper parts of your subconscious and remember. Pay attention to where you put your intention and your effort every single day. We have to collectively grow as a consciousness and take responsibility for our own actions, judgments, and expectations. When we can fully embody these old programs and uninstall them, we all collectively move forward. Any of the work you've done helps the whole. So, give yourself a little more credit, and know that, by simply reading this book and wanting the best for the collective, you are emitting a vibrational frequency that is higher than what you started with. I say with the utmost respect that I hope you find those parts of yourself that you were told to close or to be quiet about, and that you nurture them and that they emerge stronger in you because you believe in your limitlessness. Believe in your AF-ness. How AF are you? You exist in this unified field of limitlessness every single day—so ask yourself, "What would I do today if I had no fear of the unlimited?"

REFERENCES

Ashby, Muata. *The Kemetic Tree of Life: Ancient Egyptian Metaphysics & Cosmology for Higher Consciousness*. Miami: Sema Institute/Cruzian Mystic Books, 2007.

Avena, Nicole M., Pedro Rada, and Bartley G. Hoebel. "Evidence for Sugar Addiction: Behavioral and Neurochemical Effects of Intermittent, Excessive Sugar Intake." *Neuroscience & Biobehavioral Reviews* 32, no. 1 (January 2008): 20–39, https://doi.org/10.1016/j.neubiorev.2007.04.019.

Bernal, Ignacio Morgado. "Do Animals Possess Self-Awareness?" *EL PAÍS English*, August 6, 2022. english.elpais.com/science-tech/2022-08-06/do-animals-possess-self-awareness.html.

Dattani, Saloni, Fiona Spooner, Hannah Ritchie, and Max Roser. "Causes of Death." *Our World in Data*, February 14, 2018. https://ourworldindata.org/causes-of-death.

Davis, Tchiki. "Mindsets: Definition, Examples and Books on Mindset (Growth, Fixed + Other Types)." *The Berkeley Well-Being Institute*, 2017. www.berkeleywellbeing.com/mindsets.html.

Dispenza, Joe. *Becoming Supernatural How Common People Are Doing the Uncommon*. Vista, CA: Hay House, 2019.

Encyclopædia Britannica, 2020, www.britannica.com/technology/galvanometer, s.v. "galvanometer."

Encyclopædia Britannica, 2020, www.britannica.com/biography/Guido-dArezzo-Italian-musician, s.v. "Guido d'Arezzo."

Goel, Dev B., and Sarju Zilate. "Potential Therapeutic Effects of Psilocybin: A Systematic Review." *Cureus*, October 12, 2022, https://doi.org/10.7759/cureus.30214.

Johns Hopkins Medicine. "Keep Your Brain Young with Music." *Johns Hopkins Medicine*, 2019, www.hopkinsmedicine.org/health/wellness-and-prevention/keep-your-brain-young-with-music.

REFERENCES

Kramer, Samuel Noah. *The Sumerians: Their History, Culture and Character.* Chicago: University of Chicago Press, 1965.

Lagomarsino, Valentina. "Exploring the Underground Network of Trees—the Nervous System of the Forest." *Science in the News*, May 6, 2019, sitn.hms.harvard.edu/flash/2019/exploring-the-underground-network-of-trees-the-nervous-system-of-the-forest/.

Lawrence, Natalie. "The Radical New Experiments That Hint at Plant Consciousness." *New Scientist*, August 4, 2022, http://www.newscientist.com/article/mg25534012-800-the-radical-new-experiments-that-hint-at-plant-consciousness/.

Leininger, Andrea, and Bruce Leininger. *Soul Survivor.* New York: Grand Central Publishing, 2009.

Ma, Xiao, Fang Nan, Hantian Lang, Panyin Shu, Xinzou Fan, Xiaoshuang Song, Yanfeng Hou, and Dunfang Zhang. "Excessive Intake of Sugar: An Accomplice of Inflammation." *Frontiers in Immunology* 13, no. 13 (August 31, 2002), https://doi.org/10.3389/fimmu.2022.988481.

"Massage Therapy." *Cleveland Clinic.* Accessed July 24, 2023. https://my.clevelandclinic.org/departments/wellness/integrative/treatments-services/massage-therapy#reiki-tab.

McKnight, Jason. "Full List of Hospitals That Use Reiki in the US." *Planet Meditate.* https://planetmeditate.com/full-list-hospitals-that-use-reiki-us/.

McManus, David E. "Reiki Is Better than Placebo and Has Broad Potential as a Complementary Health Therapy." *Journal of Evidence-Based Complementary & Alternative Medicine* 22, no. 4 (September 5, 2017): 1051–7, https://doi.org/10.1177/2156587217728644.

Minewiser, Lorna. "Six Sessions of Emotional Freedom Techniques Remediate One Veteran's Combat-Related Post-Traumatic Stress Disorder." *Medical Acupuncture* 29, no 4 (August 2017): 249–53, https://doi.org/10.1089/acu.2017.1216. Accessed July 14, 2020.

"Number Symbolism—Pythagoreanism." *Encyclopedia Britannica*, 2005, www.britannica.com/topic/number-symbolism/Pythagoreanism, s.v. "number symbolism—Pythagoreanism."

REFERENCES

Puhan, Milo A., Alex Suarez, Christian Lo Cascio, Alfred Zahn, Markus Heitz, and Otto Braendli. "Didgeridoo Playing as Alternative Treatment for Obstructive Sleep Apnoea Syndrome: Randomised Controlled Trial." *BMJ: British Medical Journal* 332, no. 7536 (February 4, 2006): 266–70, https://doi.org/10.1136/bmj.38705.470590.55.

Reybrouck, Mark, Piotr Podlipniak, and David Welch. "Music and Noise: Same or Different? What Our Body Tells Us." *Frontiers in Psychology* 10, no. 1153 (June 25, 2019), https://doi.org/10.3389/fpsyg.2019.01153.

Shu, Frank. "Cosmology—Finite or Infinite?" *Encyclopædia Britannica*, 2020, www.britannica.com/science/cosmology-astronomy/Finite-or-infinite.

Saint Thomas, Sophie. *Glamour Witch*. Newburyport, MA: Weiser Books, 2023.

Vitale, Anne. "An Integrative Review of Reiki Touch Therapy Research." *Holistic Nursing Practice* 21, no. 4 (July 2007): 167–79, https://doi.org/10.1097/01.hnp.0000280927.83506.f6.

NOTES

Part 1: What Is a Metaphysical Mindset?

1   *A habit is a redundant set of automatic, unconscious thoughts*: Joe Dispenza, *Becoming Supernatural: How Common People Are Doing the Uncommon* (Vista, CA: Hay House, 2017).

Chapter 1: Learning from the Past

3   *In ancient civilizations like India and China*: Martin Heidegger, *Introduction to Metaphysics: Second Edition* (New Haven, CT: Yale University Press, 2014), 12–30.

3   *The Upanishads, part of the Vedic scriptures in Hinduism*: Eknath Easwaran, *Essence of the Upanishads: A Key to Indian Spirituality* (Tomales, CA: Nilgiri Press, 2009), 17.

3   *The* Bhagavad Gita, *a revered Hindu scripture*: Eknath Easwaran, *Easwaran's Classics of Indian Spirituality* (Tomales, CA: Nilgiri Press, 2007).

3   *In Chinese philosophy, the* Tao Te Ching *by Lao Tzu expounds the principles of the* Tao: Lao Tzu, *Tao Teh Ching* (Boston: Shambhala, 2006).

4   *Plato's dialogues, particularly* The Republic: Plato, *The Republic* (New York: Penguin Classics, 2007).

4   *particularly* The Republic *and* Timaeus, *investigated the nature of reality*: Plato, *Timaeus and Critias* (New York: Penguin Classics, 2008).

4   *Aristotle's* Metaphysics *examined the principles of being*: Aristotle, *The Metaphysics* (National Geographic Books, 1999).

4   *Christian theologians like St. Augustine of Hippo*: Saint Augustine, *The Confessions of Saint Augustine* (Hyde Park, NY: New City Press, 2002).

4   *Thomas Aquinas, in* Summa Theologica, *presented a comprehensive synthesis of Christian theology*: Saint Thomas Aquinas, *Summa Theologica* (Claremont, CA: Coyote Canyon Press, 2018).

4   *Renowned thinkers like René Descartes*: René Descartes, *Meditations on First Philosophy* (London: Pearson, 1951).

4   *Spinoza's* Ethics *explored the concept of God*: Benedict de Spinoza, *Ethics* (London: Penguin Classics, 1996).

4   *Leibniz's* Monadology *delved into the nature of reality*: Benedict de Spinoza, *Ethics* (London: Penguin Classics, 1996).

5   *In the nineteenth century, transcendentalist thinkers*: Ralph Waldo Emerson, *Self-Reliance* (New York: Penguin Classics, 2019).

     Henry David Thoreau, *Walden and Civil Disobedience* (New York: Penguin Classics, 1983).

5   *German idealists like Immanuel Kant*: Immanuel Kant, *Critique of Pure Reason* (London: Penguin Classics, 2007).

     Georg Wilhelm Friedrich Hegel, *Georg Wilhelm Friedrich Hegel: The Phenomenology of Spirit* (New York: Cambridge University Press, 2018).

5   *Albert Einstein's theory of relativity revolutionized our understanding of space, time, and gravity*: Albert Einstein, *Relativity: The Special and the General Theory* (New York: Fingerprint! Publishing, 2017).

5   *Carl Jung's exploration of the collective unconscious and archetypes expanded metaphysical inquiries*: C. G. Jung, *The Red Book: A Reader's Edition* (New York: W. W. Norton & Company, 2012).

5   *Contemporary philosophers and writers like Alan Watts*: Alan Watts, *The Book: On the Taboo Against Knowing Who You Are* (New York: Vintage Books, 1989).

     Ken Wilber, *A Brief History of Everything* (Shambhala Publications, 2007).

8   *In some locations there are even schools for such pursuits*: "Doctoral Program Introduction—Metaphysical Degrees Programs," *University of Metaphysics*, April 27, 2023, https://universityofmetaphysics.com/introduction/.

Chapter 2: What Is a Metaphysical Mindset?

10   *You are, in fact, a biological computer*: Joe Dispenza, *Becoming Supernatural: How Common People Are Doing the Uncommon* (Vista, CA: Hay House, 2017), 28.

10   *From the thoughts you think, to the beliefs you continue to tell yourself*: Joe Dispenza, *Becoming Supernatural: How Common People Are Doing the Uncommon* (Vista, CA: Hay House, 2017), 48.

Chapter 3: The Laws of the Universe

13   *Understanding the Laws of the Universe is the key to unlocking the power of cocreation*: Santi, *The Twelve Spiritual Laws of the Universe: A Pathway to Ascension* (Scotts Valley, CA: CreateSpace Independent Pub., 2011), 22.

13   *The bestselling book and movie,* The Secret: Rhonda Byrne, *The Secret* (New York: Simon & Schuster, 2011).

14   *Science is the empirical study of the natural world*: Steve Taylor, *Spiritual Science: Why Science Needs Spirituality to Make Sense of the World* (London: Watkins Media Limited, 2018).

Chapter 4: The Brain Is Your Best Manifesting Friend

50   *Every time you feel an emotion or you have a thought*: Joe Dispenza, *Becoming Supernatural: How Common People Are Doing the Uncommon* (Vista, CA: Hay House, 2017), 40.

51   *"If thoughts are the vocabulary of the brain . . ."*: Joe Dispenza, 2017. *Becoming Supernatural: How Common People Are Doing the Uncommon* (Vista, CA: Hay House, 2017), 48.

52   *Our bodies produce a measurable electromagnetic field*: Joe Dispenza, *Becoming Supernatural: How Common People Are Doing the Uncommon* (Vista, CA: Hay House, 2017), 49.

53   *A Harvard study took place with a group of volunteers*: Joe Dispenza, *Becoming Supernatural: How Common People Are Doing the Uncommon* (Vista, CA: Hay House, 2017), 37.

55   *When you are stressed and you have intense anxiety*: Joe Dispenza, *Becoming Supernatural: How Common People Are Doing the Uncommon* (Vista, CA: Hay House, 2017), 47.

56   *The answer is in brainwave frequencies*: Joe Dispenza, *Becoming Supernatural: How Common People Are Doing the Uncommon* (Vista, CA: Hay House, 2017), 91–93, 109–110.

57   *Binaural beats can be found all over the internet*: "Binaural Beats from Metaphysical AF," Spotify, n.d., https://open.spotify.com/playlist /0a6MzKxhtlRT3tlDhoW6bW?si=ZnMZCN88SCiGIQLochxMBg&nd=1.

57–58 *High-range beta waves can be over three times higher than low-range beta*: Joe Dispenza, *Becoming Supernatural: How Common People Are Doing the Uncommon* (Vista, CA: Hay House, 2017), 131–133.

60   *There was a French researcher named Renee Peoc'h*: Joe Dispenza, *Becoming Supernatural: How Common People Are Doing the Uncommon* (Vista, CA: Hay House, 2017), 78–79.

62   *So, what is the quantum field?*: Joe Dispenza, *Becoming Supernatural: How Common People Are Doing the Uncommon*, (Vista, CA: Hay House, 2017), 61–83.

Chapter 5: Ethereal Reminders

71   *In ancient civilizations like Mesopotamia*: Joshua J. Mark, "Ghosts in Ancient Mesopotamia," *World History Encyclopedia*, February 2023, https://www .worldhistory.org/article/2101/ghosts-in-ancient-mesopotamia/.

74–79 *Animals used as calling cards*: Ted Andrews, *Animal Speak: The Spiritual & Magical Powers of Creatures Great and Small* (Woodbury, MN: Llewellyn Worldwide, 2010), 241–300.

80   *In numerology, as in Pythagorean philosophy*: David A. Phillips, PhD., *The Complete Book of Numerology* (Vista, CA: Hay House, 2005).

Part 2: Mindset Rituals
Chapter 6: Glamorize Your Life

93   *To learn more on glamour magic, refer to the References and Resources sections*: Sophie Saint Thomas, *Glamour Witch: Conjuring Style and Grace to Get What You Want* (Newburyport, MA: Weiser Books, 2023).

Chapter 7: Alchemize Daily

100   *Alchemy is associated with experiments*: C.G. Jung, *Psychology and Alchemy* (Abingdon-on-Themes, Oxfordshire: Routledge, 2014).

NOTES

Chapter 8: Vacation at the Void

113   *A past life regression is a non-invasive form of hypnotism*: Brian L. Weiss, *Many Lives, Many Masters: The True Story of a Prominent Psychiatrist, His Young Patient, and the Past-Life Therapy That Changed Both Their Lives* (New York: Simon & Schuster, 1988).

113   *The word "Akasha" comes from an ancient Sanskrit word*: Erin Werley, *One Truth, One Law: I Am, I Create* (Hammond, IN: Madleo Publishing LLC, 2019).

114   *Everyone can do it—not just the well-informed*: Kevin J. Todeschi, *Edgar Cayce on the Akashic Records* (Virginia Beach, VA: ARE Press, 1998).

Part 3: Working with the Quantum
Chapter 9: Quantum Leaps

123   *The universe that we live in is three-dimensional*: Michio Kaku, *Quantum Supremacy: How Quantum Computers Will Unlock the Mysteries of Science—and Address Humanity's Biggest Challenges* (New York: Random House, 2023), 31–33.

124   *This is exactly how Newtonian physics describes the measurement of time*: Gale E. Christianson, *Isaac Newton* (New York: Oxford University Press, 2005).

126   *Some studies Dr. Joe Dispenza and his team have done*: Joe Dispenza, *Becoming Supernatural: How Common People Are Doing the Uncommon* (Vista, CA: Hay House, 2017), 109–111.

Chapter 10: Energetic Bodywork

135   *Many people consider Reiki a pseudoscience*: "Massage Therapy," *Cleveland Clinic,* n.d., https://my.clevelandclinic.org/departments/wellness/integrative/treatments-services/massage-therapy#reiki-tab.

135   *Today, the number one leading cause of death in the United States is heart disease*: Saloni Dattani, Fiona Spooner, Hannah Ritchie, and Max Roser, "Causes of Death," *Our World in Data*, February 14, 2018, https://ourworldindata.org/causes-of-death.

135   *Even for those who doubt the science behind Reiki*: Ellen Hanson, Leslie A. Kalish, Emily Bunce, Christine Curtis, Samuel McDaniel, Janice Ware, and Judith J. Petry, "Use of Complementary and Alternative Medicine among Children Diagnosed with Autism Spectrum Disorder," *Journal of Autism and*

Developmental Disorders 37, no. 4, 2006, Springer Science+Business Media: 628–36. https://doi.org/10.1007/s10803–006–0192–0.

Marie N. Bremner, Barbara J. Blake, Viqi Wagner, and Sharon M. Pearcey, "Effects of Reiki with Music Compared to Music Only among People Living with HIV," *Journal of the Association of Nurses in AIDS Care* 27, no. 5, 2016: 635–47. https://doi.org/10.1016/j.jana.2016.04.004.

M. L. Morse and Lance W. Beem, "Benefits of *Reiki* Therapy for a Severely Neutropenic Patient with Associated Influences on a True Random Number Generator," *Journal of Alternative and Complementary Medicine* 17, no. 12, 2011. Mary Ann Liebert, Inc.: 1181–90. https://doi.org/10.1089/acm.2010.0238.

David E. McManus, "Reiki Is Better than Placebo and Has Broad Potential as a Complementary Health Therapy," *Journal of Evidence-Based Complementary & Alternative Medicine* 22, no. 4, 2017, SAGE Publishing: 1051–57. https://doi.org/10.1177/2156587217728644.

Anne Vitale, "An Integrative Review of Reiki Touch Therapy Research." *Holistic Nursing Practice* 21 no. 4, 2007. Lippincott Williams & Wilkins: 167–79. https://doi.org/10.1097/01.hnp.0000280927.83506.f6.

135 *Reiki is derived from the Japanese words "rei"*: Diane Stein, *Essential Reiki: A Complete Guide to an Ancient Healing Art* (Berkeley, CA: Crossing Press, 2011).

136 *Reiki is not specific to any type of disease or condition.* Ann Baldwin, *Reiki in Clinical Practice: A Science-Based Guide* (Edinburgh: Handspring Publishing, 2020).

139 *Emotional Freedom Technique is self-help practice*: Nick Ortner, *The Tapping Solution* (Vista, CA: Hay House, 2013).

140 *In the* Law of Attraction *books by Esther Hicks*: Esther Hicks and Jerry Hicks, *The Law of Attraction: The Basics of the Teachings of Abraham* (Carlsbad, CA: Hay House, 2006).

143 *a galvanometer, which can not only detect the precise locations of acupressure points, but also help determine energy buildup*: "Galvanometer: Voltage, Current & Resistance," Encyclopedia Britannica, July 20, 1998, https://www.britannica.com/technology/galvanometer.

144 *EFT was first studied with war veterans*: Lorna Minewiser, "Six Sessions of Emotional Freedom Techniques Remediate One Veteran's Combat-Related Post-Traumatic Stress Disorder," *Medical Acupuncture* 29, no. 4, 2017. Mary Ann Liebert, Inc.: 249–53. https://doi.org/10.1089/acu.2017.1216.

Chapter 11: Healing beyond Boundaries

148 *The term "somatic" means "relating to the body"*: Susan McConnell Cifst, *Somatic Internal Family Systems Therapy: Awareness, Breath, Resonance, Movement and Touch in Practice* (Berkeley, CA: North Atlantic Books, 2020).

148 *There are many techniques that a somatic therapist can use*: Sidney H. Kennedy and Peter Giacobbe, "Treatment Resistant Depression—Advances in Somatic Therapies," *Annals of Clinical Psychiatry* 19, no. 4, 2007: 279–87. https://doi.org/10.1080/10401230701675222.

152 *Sound healing combined with somatic therapy*: George L. Engel, "The Need for a New Medical Model: A Challenge for Biomedicine," *Science* 196, no. 4286, 1977: 129–36. https://doi.org/10.1126/science.847460.

153 *Studies have shown that vibrational forces of sound*: Mark Reybrouck, Piotr Podlipniak, and David Welch. "Music and Noise: Same or Different? What Our Body Tells Us," *Frontiers in Psychology* 10, June 2019, https://doi.org/10.3389/fpsyg.2019.01153.

153 *This has been suggested to improve metabolism*: "Music and Noise: Same or Different? What Our Body Tells Us," *Frontiers in Psychology* 10, June 2019, https://doi.org/10.3389/fpsyg.2019.01153.

153 *This is because when we listen to music*: "Keep Your Brain Young with Music," *Johns Hopkins Medicine,* April 13, 2022, https://www.hopkinsmedicine.org/health/wellness-and-prevention/keep-your-brain-young-with-music.

156 *Originally there was a twelve-note annotation scale*: "Guido d'Arezzo: Medieval Music Theory, Notation & Hymns," *Encyclopedia Britannica,* July 20, 1998, https://www.britannica.com/biography/Guido-dArezzo-Italian-musician.

157 *However, in 2005, the British medical journal discovered*: Milo A. Puhan, Alex Suarez, Christian Lo Cascio, Alfred Zahn, Markus Heitz, and Otto Braendli,

"Didgeridoo Playing as Alternative Treatment for Obstructive Sleep Apnoea Syndrome: Randomised Controlled Trial," *British Medical Journal* 332, no. 7536, 2005: 266–70. doi:10.1136/bmj.38705.470590.55.

Part 4: The Companion Kingdoms
Chapter 12: Animal Energy

167 *Spirit guides, spirit animals, power animals*: Steven D. Farmer, PhD, *Animal Spirit Guides* (Vista, CA: Hay House, 2006).

168 *Keep in mind that every animal has a specific symbolic meaning*: Ted Andrews, *Animal Speak: The Spiritual & Magical Powers of Creatures Great and Small* (Woodbury, MN: Llewellyn Worldwide, 2010), 4–7.

Chapter 13: Crystal Beings

175 *We are aware that plants can react to stimuli*: Natalie Lawrence, "The Radical New Experiments That Hint at Plant Consciousness," *New Scientist*, August 2022, https://www.newscientist.com/article/mg25534012-800-the-radical-new-experiments-that-hint-at-plant-consciousness/.

175 *species as diverse as cats, chimpanzees, and dolphins*: Ignacio Morgado Bernal, "Do Animals Possess Self-Awareness?" *EL PAÍS English*, August 6, 2022, https://english.elpais.com/science-tech/2022-08-06/do-animals-possess-self-awareness.html.

Chapter 14: Mycelium: The Earth's Neural Network

180 *Under your feet is an entire network of interconnected cells*: SITNFlash, "Exploring The Underground Network of Trees—The Nervous System of the Forest—Science in the News," *Science in the News,* March 24, 2022, https://sitn.hms.harvard.edu/flash/2019/exploring-the-underground-network-of-trees-the-nervous-system-of-the-forest/.

181 *Research suggests that psilocybin-assisted therapy may be effective*: Dev B. Goel and Sarju Zilate, "Potential Therapeutic Effects of Psilocybin: A Systematic Review," *Cureus*, October 2022, https://doi.org/10.7759/cureus.30214.

Chapter 15: Plant Spirit Medicine

190 *The year was 2017, and I was living in Denver, Colorado*: Ashley Manta, "A Night of Exploration and Empowerment: Green Lodge Goddess Gathering

Debuts in LA," *DOPE Magazine*, July 26, 2017, https://tv.dopemagazine.com /green-lodge-goddess-la/.

Chapter 16: Psychedelic Plant Spirits

201 *When an individual eats sugar*: Nicole M. Avena, Pedro Rada, and Bartley G. Hoebel, "Evidence for Sugar Addiction: Behavioral and Neurochemical Effects of Intermittent, Excessive Sugar Intake," *Neuroscience & Biobehavioral Reviews* 32, no. 1, 2008: 20–39, https://doi.org/10.1016/j.neubiorev.2007.04.019.

Conclusion: Being Metaphysical

218 *expanded on the knowledge in the* Metaphysical Cannabis Oracle Deck: Maggie Wilson, *The Metaphysical Cannabis Oracle Deck* (New York: Union Square & Co., 2022).

RESOURCES

Here are some tools that have helped me so much in my own journey toward becoming metaphysical AF. I hope they're as useful for you as they were for me.

BOOKS

Glamour Magic: The Witchcraft Revolution to Get What You Want
by Deborah Castellano

Enchantments: A Modern Witch's Guide to Self-Possession by Mya Spalter

The Power of Now: A Guide to Spiritual Enlightenment by Eckhart Tolle

The Kybalion: Hermetic Philosophy by The Three Initiates

The Secret Teachings of All Ages by Manly P. Hall

The Tarot Bible: The Definitive Guide to the Cards and Spreads by Sarah Bartlett

The Complete Book of Tarot Reversals by Mary K. Greer

Holistic Tarot: An Integrative Approach to Using Tarot for Personal Growth
by Benebell Wen

The Only Astrology Book You'll Ever Need by Joanna Martine Woolfolk

Astrology for the Soul by Jan Spiller

The Modern Witchcraft Book of Astrology: Your Guide to the Stars by Skye Alexander

Becoming Supernatural: How Common People Are Doing the Uncommon
by Dr. Joe Dispenza

The Power of Intention: Learning to Co-create Your World Your Way by
Dr. Wayne W. Dyer

You Can Heal Your Life by Louise Hay

The Tarot Coloring Book by Theresa Reed

Finding Your Higher Self: Your Guide to Cannabis for Self-Care by Sophie Saint Thomas

Inner Witch: A Modern Guide to the Ancient Craft by Gabriela Herstik

Animal Speak: The Spiritual & Magical Powers of Creatures Great & Small by Ted Andrews

The Complete Book of Dreams by Tony Crisp

The Secret History of the World by Mark Booth

The Disappearance of the Universe by Gary Renard

ONLINE PLATFORMS

Gaia: Streaming platform with a vast library of metaphysical content, documentaries, and teachings. https://www.gaia.com/

AstroStyle: Astrology platform founded by the AstroTwins, offering daily horoscopes and astrological insights. https://astrostyle.com/

Astrology King: Astrology platform offering planetary guidance and horoscopes. https://astrologyking.com/

AstroSeek: Online astrology resource with free birth charts, interpretations, and learning tools. https://www.astro-seek.com/

MindBodyGreen: Wellness platform featuring articles, courses, and expert advice on holistic health and spirituality. https://www.mindbodygreen.com/

Bustle: Lifestyle platform featuring great articles on wellness and spirituality. https://www.bustle.com/

Mindvalley: Offers online courses on personal growth, spirituality, and transformation, with a focus on expanding consciousness. https://www.mindvalley.com/

PODCASTS

Metaphysical As F***: Aka my podcast! *Metaphysical As F**** dives into the truth behind your unleashed powers, how your body and brain work beyond this physical realm, and how being authentic AF is the key to happiness.

The Resilient Mind: A podcast that features global thought leaders on the topics of spirituality and metaphysics.

Metaphysical Milkshake: Hosted by Rainn Wilson and scholar Reza Aslan, this podcast gives weekly insight into the realm of metaphysics with a comedic take.

MUSIC FESTIVALS

Jam Cruise: Jam Cruise sails through the Caribbean, leaving from Miami, Florida, every year, hosting over thirty bands on eight stages, and it includes great wellness activities. This is a one-of-a-kind music festival that has become my favorite. https://jamcruise.com/

Same Same But Different: A lakeside music festival happening in Southern California promoting wellness and camaraderie. The thought and intention that goes into this festival and the wellness programming is exceptional. Highly recommended. https://www.ssbdfest.com/

Envision Festival: A seven-day festival in the heart of the Costa Rican jungle with live music, arts, and wellness activities. A bucket list *must* for all music festival lovers. https://www.envisionfestival.com/

Suwanne Hulaween: Suwannee Hulaween is an annual music and camping festival held over Halloween weekend at the Spirit of the Suwannee Music Park in Live Oak, Florida, with an extensive wellness program. https://suwanneehulaween.com/

Lightning in a Bottle: Lightning in a Bottle (LIB) is an annual music festival in the Central Valley region of California. It is presented by The Do LaB, which seeks to promote sustainability, social cohesion, and creative expression. The wellness workshops are offered to kids and teens as well. https://www.libfestival.org/

Desert Hearts: Desert Hearts Festival is one of the world's most beloved house and techno parties happening in California. The workshops and community are centered on growth and communication resulting in powerful experiences within safe spaces. https://festival.deserthearts.us/

ACKNOWLEDGMENTS

The conception of *Metaphysical AF* developed over time from being a book just about witchcraft and a cultism to a full-fledged quantum physics explanation of why manifestation is more than just a buzzword. I would not even I have been able to pitch this book and share this idea if it wasn't for the incredible author Gabriella Herstik and her unbelievable agent Jill Marr. It was Jill who inspired me to pitch this book and really supported me through the process from draft to pitch! Infinite possibility unlocked thanks to you two!

It takes a strong-minded individual to come into a space that you know no one in and pitch yourself as an expert and be able to prove that you can deliver a work that will help inspire people and create buzz that our society and culture hasn't seen before. The enormous success of *The Metaphysical Cannabis Oracle Deck* and the overwhelming support that they have given it throughout the entire world is a huge part of the inspiration for how this book truly came to life. I want to express my sincere gratitude to the team at Union Square for their trust, belief, and confidence in me. It is truly an honor to work with an incredible team that continues to create a space in the world that aligns with my own values. Thank you everyone, especially Kate Z.

I would like to thank my incredible spiritual support group and the deepest friends I have truly ever known, who continue to inspire me and cheered me on to complete this book and deliver it to the world: Katie, Nicole, Jamie, Brett, Joslyn, Diana, Nina, Kristen, Ashley, Natalie, David, Miranda, Stephanie, Mackenzie, Lauren, Kate, Evan, Arturo, Meredith, Izzy, Daniel, Sailene, Ricco, Philip, Cola, Ali, Shannon, Emily, Savvy, Gregory, Evan, Chantal, Noemi, CeeCee, Brittany,

ACKNOWLEDGMENTS

and Madison. Thanks to every single dog I encountered, who truly made my soul happy, including Lola Belle Jenkins and my favorite angel bulldog, Cash.

My lifelong friends and constant support system, Ashley T. and Stephanie G.: I wouldn't have had the courage to be my weird self without you. Thank you both for always showing me what true strength and creativity can do. I can't wait to see where life takes you.

I'd like to express a huge thank-you to Joe Moore of *Psychedelics Today* for his dedication to the community and for reminding me that the soul sees you before anything else. I am grateful for our time together in one of the most magical spaces to let our soul's shine.

Thank you to Jamie Wollberg for being the sounding board, body double, and guide I needed when shifts took place in my life during this process. I know I can always count on you to be there to listen with compassion and unconditional love.

To Katie, I wish we met when we were fifteen so we could have grown up listening to Taylor Swift together, but I'm grateful we met in our late twenties and spent a night bonding on a Greyhound Bus from Oakland to Los Angeles while listening to *My Favorite Murder*. You inspire me and give me strength and I hope to always make you laugh. Thank you for always holding space for me when I couldn't hold it myself. I'm sure somehow my mom and your dad met in another plane and are having a great time cheering us on.

Deep, heartfelt gratitude to Nina Grae—we started talking about these things happening years ago on that Santa Monica rooftop! My songbird sister from another lifetime, you bring me so much joy when we talk and spend time together. Your grace alone is a quality I channel daily, and I am blessed to have your friendship.

I have to thank the incredible soul Natalie for meeting me and my partner on top of the Uxmal Temple of the Magician and snapping our photo, because I never knew I could bond with someone so fast! Your friendship and ability to go beyond my hopes and dreams will always be something I carry with me. Thank you for helping me move, being with me through the hardest times, and dancing with me during the best. We'll dance until we are old ladies!

My ride or reincarnated, Alex M., your support has been unending since day one, when we met in the Coachella Valley. I knew when I moved to California that you would be one of my closest friends and you stepped up to the plate long before I even realized. Thank you for your endless support. You show me that no matter what life throws at you, our motto is always, "I'm going to be okay." I love you for that, because you're so incredibly right.

To my now-husband, Brandon: my gratitude for you knows the farthest reaches of time and space. From the moment we met, I believed in you, in us, and in everything we were going to do together. You truly are my best friend, the love of my life, and everything I always wanted in a partner. I'm honored to be your wife and stand by your side. You are a genius and talented beyond this realm. I love that I get to spend a lifetime hearing your playlists and dancing into the sunrise with you.

To my children, Achilles and Aurora, who have given me some of the best, most magical moments of my life: you are growing up faster than I realized, with your own unique and powerful gifts. You are the kindest and most precious souls I have ever known. It has been an honor to be your mother and I am so proud of you both. I can't wait to see what you do with your lives and how you share your gifts. I will always cheer you on because I am always with you.

As a last note, I would like to acknowledge the community behind the Green Lodge, *The Metaphysical AF* podcast, and all the students and clients I've worked with over the years. I am truly inspired and empowered by all of you. You are literally metaphysical AF!

INDEX

Action. *See* Inspired action, law of
Addictions, 23, 24, 54–55
Affirmations
  for radiant glamour ritual, 95
  used in EFT tapping, 139–40
Akashic records
  about: reincarnation and, 108–9
  astral travel and, 179
  benefits of accessing, 115–16
  Chantal (guide) and, 116–17, 118
  crystals for, 179
  defined, 109, 113–14
  Google analogy, 114
  guide to help access, 115, 116–17
  information contained in,
    114–15, 116
  karmic lesson from, 117
  questions to ask, 118
  vibrational frequency and
    communicating with, 118–19
  working with, 117, 118–19
Alchemy, spiritual, 100–107
  about: overview of, 100
  benefits of, 100, 105
  daily life, chores and, 102–7
  establishing new patterns with,
    100, 101
  everyday meditation for, 103–5
  folding clothes example, 102–3
  meditation of renewal, 106–7
  questions to ask yourself,
    considerations for, 100–101
Ancestral connections, crystals
  for, 178
Animal energy, 164–74. *See also*
  Calling cards
  about: animal totems and,
    165–66; divine presence in
    nature and, 164–65
  alternative names for
    totems, 167–68
  animal colors and related
    attributes (positive/
    negative), 172
  animal directions and their
    indications, 173

animals you see the most and, 167
  attacked or bitten by animal
    and, 166
  discovering energies that will be
    your wtotems, 166–73
  dreams of animals and, 166
  exercise to meet your spirit
    animal, 168–69
  fascination level with animals
    and, 167–68
  fear-inducing experiences
    and, 167
  guiding principles, 168
  meditation (animal
    spirit), 170–71
  questions to ask to discover your
    totems, 166–67
  wolf energy and encounters
    anecdote, 174
  zoo experiences and, 167
Aquinas, Thomas, 4
Aristotle, 4
"As above, so below," 25, 165
Astral travel, 179
Attraction, law of. *See also* Inspired
  action, law of
  about, 13, 28–30
  daily gratitude and reflection, 30
  "gratitude rampage" and, 140–41
  Human Design type and, 29, 31
  journal prompt, 30
  manifesting and, 30, 91 (*See
    also* Manifesting)
  The Secret (book/movie) and, 13
Augustine of Hippo, St., 4
Awareness, opening, 182
Ayahuasca, 196, 201, 202

Balance (or gender), law of
  about, 46–48, 56
  daily gratitude and reflection, 48
  journal prompt, 48
  masculine/feminine energy and
    yin/yang, 46–48
Bats, calling cards from, 74–75
Bears, calling cards from, 75

Becoming Supernatural (Dispenza),
  26–27, 51, 87, 108, 121
Berezin, Alexander, 175
Bison, calling cards from, 75–76
Blavatsky, Helena P., 25
Body awareness, 150
Bonnie method, 154
Brain and manifesting.
  See also Manifesting;
    Quantum collapsing
  about: overview of, 50
  brain waves and, 56–60; alpha
    waves, 58; beta waves, 56–58;
    gamma waves, 58–59; theta
    waves, 58
  changing your reality, 60–62
  computer analogy, 51
  creating from the
    unknown, 51–52
  electromagnetic/light energies
    and, 52–53
  from ethereal to physical, 50–51
  fight-or-flight and, 55–56, 142
  how brain functions, 50–51
  power thoughts, emotions
    and, 54–55 (*See also*
    Emotions; Thoughts)
  studies showing
    correlation, 53–54

Calling cards
  about: decoding, 68; as ethereal
    reminders, 67, 71–74; forms
    of, 67–68; recognizing/
    understanding significance
    of, 67–68
  author's experiences, 71
  Brett's experiences, 68–70, 73
  Meredith's story, 73
  Natalie's story, 72
  Shannon's story, 72
Calling cards, animal
  about: messages from, 74 (*See
    also specific animals*)
  bats, 74–75
  bears, 75

238

INDEX

INDEX

INDEX

Intuitive work, crystals and, 179
Isotopicity, 175–76

Journal prompts
about: benefits of journaling,
15–16; daily gratitude and,
15 (*See also* Daily gratitude
and reflection); journaling
guidelines, 15; reflection after
meditation, 183
Law of Attraction, 30
Law of Balance (or Gender), 48
Law of Cause and Effect
(Karma), 38
Law of Compensation, 40
Law of Correspondence, 28
Law of Inspired Action, 33
Law of Oneness, 21
Law of Perpetual Transmutation
of Energy, 36
Law of Polarity, 44
Law of Relativity, 43
Law of Rhythm (or Perpetual
Motion), 46
Law of Vibration, 25
Judgment
animal fears indicating, 167
awareness of yours, bears and, 75
casting, 23, 24
forgiving other for, 42 (*See
also* Forgiveness)
Law of Relativity and, 40–41, 42
no judgment, no expectation, 37
psilocybin meditation
and, 184–85
releasing, 138–39, 212, 214, 216
staying in the moment, Hakomi
and, 150
taking responsibility for, 219
Jung, Carl, 5

Karma. *See* Cause and effect
(karma), law of
Kingdoms, other. *See*
Companion kingdoms

Lao Tzu, 3–4
Law of Attraction (Hicks), 140–41
Laws of the Universe
about: journaling practice and,
15–16; meditation for, 49;
overview of, 13; science,
spirituality, metaphysics, and,

14–15; value of understanding,
13, 15
Law of Attraction, 13, 28–30,
91, 140–41
Law of Balance (or Gender),
46–48, 56
Law of Cause and Effect
(Karma), 36–38
Law of Compensation, 38–40
Law of Correspondence,
25–28, 165
Law of Inspired Action, 31–33
Law of Oneness, 16–21, 62
Law of Perpetual Transmutation
of Energy, 33–36
Law of Polarity, 43–44
Law of Relativity, 40–43
Law of Rhythm (or Perpetual
Motion), 44–46, 50
Law of Vibration, 22–25
Levine, Peter A., 151–52
Listening, silent, 183

Manifesting. *See also* Brain
and manifesting
becoming infinite and, 128–29
bringing ethereal to physical
realm, 64–66
glamour of, 91–92
love-of-my-life manifestation
story, 190–98
quantum manifestation
meditation, 130–31
Medieval faith and reason, 4
Meditation
about: brain waves and, 58–59
for alchemizing daily life, 103–5
animal spirit, 170–71
bringing ethereal to physical
realm, 64–66
crystals for, 178
glamour, 98–99
grounding, 182
for Laws of the Universe, 49
manifesting, quantum collapsing
and, 62–63 (*See also*
Quantum collapsing)
psilocybin, 184–85
for psychedelic plant spirit work
on dimensional level, 204–7
quantum manifestation, 130–31
of renewal, sweeping path of
clarity, 106–7

sound healing and mantras, 154
Meditations on First Philosophy
(Descartes), 4
Memory, crystals and, 176–77
Metaphysical Cannabis Oracle Deck
(Wilson), xi, 160, 198, 218
Metaphysical intentions
about: guidelines for using, 208
itemized list of, 209–16
Metaphysics. *See also*
Historical perspective
about: being metaphysical going
forward, 217–19; overview and
summary of, this book and,
ix–xi, 1
benefits of studying, 6–8
contextual understanding, 6
grounding in traditions, 7
identification of patterns, 6–7
inspiration for personal
transformation, 7
integration of wisdom, 6
related studies to pursue, 8
relevance to contemporary
life, 7
rich heritage of ideas, 6
Metaphysics (Aristotle), 4
Mindset, metaphysical. *See also*
Brain and manifesting;
Calling cards; Laws of
the Universe
challenges and responsibilities of
embracing, 12
defined, 9
innate validation and, 11
input and output
importance, 10–11
non-metaphysical mindset
vs., 9–10
in our DNA, x, 11–12, 54, 146
shift to self-reliance and, 11–12
vision of possibilities using, 10
Modern and contemporary
explorations, 5
Monadology (Leibniz), 4
Moore, Joe, 196–97
Mushrooms, message from, 203. *See
also* Mycelium
Mycelium, 180–85. *See also*
Psilocybin
about: network of
interconnectedness
and, 180–81

INDEX

Mycelium (*continued*)
connecting with network of, 182–83
functions of, 181
gratitude, connection and, 183
grounding meditation, 182
intention-setting and, 183
journal reflection, 183
lessons from, 180–81
mushroom message, 203
opening awareness, 182
psilocybin and, 181–82, 184–85
silent listening and, 183

Native American flute, 157
Neurological Music Therapy (NMT), 154–55
Neurosomatic therapy, 151
Newtonian physics realities, 124–26. *See also* Quantum leaps
Nine, symbolism of, 84–85
NMT (Neurological Music Therapy), 154–55
Numerology, about, 79–80. *See also* Calling cards, numerical

Oneness, law of
about, 16–21
daily gratitude and reflection, 21
journal prompt, 21
magnetic charge of heart and, 18–20
manifesting and, 62–63
One, symbolism of, 81
Outputs and inputs, mental, 10–11

Past-life regression
about: reincarnation and, 108–9
author's experience, 109–12
remembering birth, 111
vacation at the void, 111–13
Patterns, identification of, 6–7
Pendulation, 149
Peoc'h, René, 60–61
Perpetual motion. *See* Rhythm (or perpetual motion), law of
Perpetual transmutation of energy, law of
about, 33–35
change as only constant and, 34
daily gratitude and reflection, 36
example, 36
journal prompt, 36

transmuting lower vibrations, 36
water example, 34
Plant-spirit medicine, 186–98. *See also* Psychedelic plant spirits
approaching plants with grace and appreciation, 188
continuing relationship with spirit, 190
electromagnetic signals from plants and, 186–88
gratitude and offerings, 190
integration and, 196–97
intentional practice of, 186
love-of-my-life manifestation story, 190–98
meditative connection and, 189
mindful observation and, 189
purification, preparation and, 200–201
receiving, interpreting messages, 189–90
Reiki and, 187
researching, choosing plant, 188
respectful communication and, 189
sacred space for, 189
sugar and, 200–201
working with plant spirits, 188–90
world spirits of plants and, 201
your truth, plant's message and, 201–2
Plato, 4
Polarity, law of
about, 43–44
daily gratitude and reflection, 44
journal prompt, 44
Psilocybin. *See also* Mycelium
about: author's background, experiences and, 160–63
meditation, 184–85
psychedelic experience induced by, 181–82
what it is, how it works, 181
Psychedelic plant spirits, 199–207. *See also* Psilocybin
about: author's background, experiences and, 160–63; guidelines, disclaimer on working with, 199
Ayahuasca message, 202
cactus message, 202–3

cannabis message, 203–4
channeling and hearing message, 200
meditation to work with on a dimensional level (6 dimensions), 204–7
mushrooms' message, 203
no judgment, no expectation and, 199
setting intention, 200
Psychedelics Today podcast, 196–97
Pythagoras, numerology and, 79–80. *See also* Calling cards, numerical

Quantum
about: working with, 121–22
experiences within, 126–29
manifestation meditation, 130–31
reaching, 126–27 (*See also* Quantum leaps)
reality within, 128–29
space, time and, 123–24, 126
vision when experiencing, 126–27
Quantum collapsing
about: overview of manifesting and, 30; transcending limits and, 60
explained, 59–60, 62–63
fully understanding, 125
how to change your reality and, 60–61
intention causing, 62–63
manifesting and, 62–63, 64–66
requirement for, 60
tapping infinite potential, 60
Quantum leaps
about: overview of, 123; working with the quantum, 121–22
becoming infinite, 128–29
Newtonian physics realities and, 124–26
reaching and experiencing the quantum, 126–29
space, time and, 123–24, 126

Rain sticks, 157
Reality
changing, baby chicks study illustrating, 60–61
how to change yours, 60–62
Reflections, daily. *See* Daily gratitude and reflection

242

INDEX

ABOUT THE AUTHOR

Maggie Wilson, originally from Tennessee and now based in California, is a globally recognized metaphysical expert and Reiki master. Her profound insights have resonated across the world, as celebrated by notable features in *Best Life, Bustle, Insider, Forbes, MindBodyGreen,* and the *New York Times.* Maggie, a loving mother of two, finds her inspiration in her journey through motherhood and adds depth and relatability to her insights, making her guidance even more powerful and resonant. She is also the author and creator behind the widely acclaimed *Metaphysical Cannabis Oracle Deck,* a transformative tool that illuminates pathways to self-discovery and profound healing. This is her first book. Visit beacons.ai/wilsonmaggie and metaphysicalaf.com to follow and learn more.